RAZOR-WIRE
DHARMA

CALVIN MALONE

RAZOR-WIRE DHARMA

A BUDDHIST LIFE IN PRISON

Foreword by
Steven C. Rockefeller

 WISDOM PUBLICATIONS • BOSTON

Wisdom Publications, Inc.
199 Elm Street
Somerville MA 02144 USA
www.wisdompubs.org

Library of Congress Cataloging-in-Publication Data
Malone, Calvin, 1951-
Razor-wire dharma : a Buddhist lilfe in prison / Calvin Malone.
    p. cm.
ISBN 0-86171-563-2 (pbk. : alk. paper)
1. Religious life—Buddhism. 2. Prisoners—Religious life—United States. 3.
Malone, Calvin, 1951-—Imprisonment. I1. Title.
BQ4580.P75M35 2008
294.3092—DC22
[B]
                                      2008016711

12 11 10 09 08
5 4 3 2 1

Cover design by Philip Pascuzzo. Interior design by Dede Cummings. Set in
Sabon 11.5/16.

Wisdom Publications' books are printed on acid-free paper and meet
the guidelines for permanence and durability of the Production
Guidelines for Book Longevity of the Council on Library Resources.

Printed in the United States of America.

This book was produced with environmental mindfulness. We have
elected to print this title on 30% PCW recycled paper. As a result, we
have saved the following resources: 19 trees, 13 million BTUs of energy, 1,662
lbs. of greenhouse gases, 6,900 gallons of water, and 886 lbs. of solid waste.
For more information, please visit our website, www.wisdompubs.org. This
paper is also FSC certified. For more information, please visit www.fscus.org.

Dedicated to the four people
whose enthusiasm for this book
encouraged me to never give up:

My mother,
Eleanor Mussen
For always being there

Sensei Sunyana Graef
For all those years of support

Zen Priest Vanja Palmers
For believing in me

Shane Kellberg
For loyalty and devotion

CONTENTS

Foreword   ix
Editor's Preface   xi
Acknowledgments   xvii
Introduction   1

Entering the Way   9
The Abyss   29
Eyeball   43
Banana   47
Forty-Nine   55
Bulldog and Christmas   65
A Little Closer to Home   71
Essential Oil   79
Anger   85

Getting Involved   91
Derrick   95
Soup   103
Munny   109
The Reluctant Zen Master   119
Tying Flies   131
Apple   135
Hacksaw   139
Shawn   147
Artichoke Heart   159
Metta   165
Freedom   169
A Close Encounter   171
Letting Go   173
Happy Holidays   177
Miracles   179
Liberating Our Gardens   181
Postscripts   185
Author's Note   189

APPENDIXES

I. The Four Noble Truths   193
II. Meditation   199
III. Recommended Reading   215
IV. Resource Guide   219

About the Author   227

FOREWORD

In *Razor-Wire Dharma* Calvin Malone provides a convincing and moving account of his spiritual awakening and how it transformed his way of living and relating to others. That his spiritual odyssey takes place while he is serving an extended sentence in the Washington State prison system makes his story particularly compelling and significant. *Razor-Wire Dharma* also provides a valuable introduction to the nature and purpose of Buddhist practice, and Calvin's commitment and courage will be a challenging inspiration to those who are already following the Buddhist path.

Buddhism offers people practical wisdom and provides them with a practice that promotes intellectual, emotional, and spiritual growth. It can change how people think and behave. It is not a magical cure-all, and there are no short cuts. Serious Buddhist practice is a demanding discipline that requires hard work, courage, and perseverance. The rewards are inner freedom and peace and discovery of the joy that can be found in caring relationships and in the contemplation of things like an apple or a pine tree.

Calvin's stories are an especially good introduction to Buddhism, because they make clear that Buddhist spiritual practice involves much more than sitting meditation, important as this is. In the Mahayana Buddhist tradition, meditation is preparation for going forth into the world. Responding to the suffering and needs of others with understanding and compassion is the deeper meaning of practice. At the heart of Buddhist teaching are two guiding principles: Help others, and if you cannot help others, Do not harm them. This is the bodhisattva path.

The most important factor in Calvin's transformation is his own determined quest for freedom and wholeness. However, he sought guidance and support outside the prison system in the American Buddhist community, and he received it. Among those Buddhist teachers who responded was Sunyana Graef, and she assisted Calvin as he developed the manuscript for this book. Sensei Graef's teacher was Roshi Philip Kapleau. He was among the small vanguard of Americans who went to Asia for extended Buddhist training in the 1950s and 1960s and then introduced authentic Buddhist practice and the bodhisattva ideal to Americans. Both Sensei Graef's work as a Zen teacher and Calvin's Buddhist life in prison grow from seeds planted by Roshi Kapleau. Somewhere there is a gentle smile on Roshi's face, and I can hear his harmonica playing.

Steven C. Rockefeller is Professor Emeritus of Religion at Middlebury College in Vermont.

EDITOR'S PREFACE

YEARS AGO I was talking with my teacher, Roshi Philip Kapleau, about making a sacrifice that might harm oneself but would definitely help someone else. I asked him what he would do in such a situation. He had been practicing Zen Buddhism for over forty years and I was sure I knew the answer—before he could say a word I blurted out, "You'd act immediately, Roshi, without thinking twice!" He looked at me, then looked down without saying a word. A minute later he replied, softly, slowly: "I'd like to think I would."

My teacher's humility has come back to me many times through the years, never more so than when I read Calvin Malone's stories. It takes courage and conviction to make choices that place the welfare of others before our own. Those of us practicing a spiritual discipline that emphasizes the bodhisattva ideal of liberating all sentient beings hope our responses under duress will be compassionate and wise, selfless and loving. But we don't honestly know what they will be—few of us ever find ourselves in the kinds of situations that would test us in that way.

How would we react if confronted by a knife-wielding assassin, an enraged maniac, a lying thief, a desperate young man needing protection from thugs? What if the compassionate choice would disrupt our comfort and put us directly in harm's way? In prison, the only place Calvin has ever encountered and practiced the Dharma, these are not hypothetical questions. Your safety, your welfare, your peace of mind is never a given behind bars and your response to a situation can be, quite literally, a life-or-death choice—for you or someone else.

It has been my privilege to work with Calvin preparing his material for publication. The stories range in time from before Calvin's incarceration through the present and were written during the course of fifteen years in different Washington State prisons. The accounts in the book are true, but the names of people have been changed—although to a person the prisoners profiled at length told Calvin they felt honored to be included in his book.

As you read Calvin's stories, you may wonder how you would have met the challenges that came to him in prison. I certainly have. Calvin first contacted me in 1992 and began sending his writings not long afterward. Sometimes they were asides in handwritten letters—"Last week a funny thing happened" (followed by the story which appears as "Apple")—sometimes they were carefully typed accounts that stood on their own. I was stunned by the power and courage of his tales. They were riveting, inspiring, honest. Often I was moved to read his words in Zen talks to my students, and many of them found their way into our monthly newsletter and those of other Buddhist groups. Each story was a gift from someone who truly took the Dharma to heart.

Calvin, by his own admission, was a violent and angry person when he entered prison. His transformation, therefore, when it came, was all that much more dramatic. Nonetheless, it is only natural to wonder whether some of the situations he relates and his responses to them could possibly be true. Since I wasn't an eye-witness to any of the events Calvin writes about, I base the accuracy of these stories on my knowledge of Calvin through our years of correspondence, a few phone calls, a couple of visits, and the testimony of others (primarily West Coast Buddhist teachers) who have had more opportunities for face-to-face contact with Calvin than I have.

But the most compelling evidence comes from the numerous people Calvin has helped over the years who have written to me for one reason or another. Letter after letter bears witness to Calvin's generosity and compassion. A Cambodian inmate encloses a letter from his lawyer with the news of winning his INS trial. Without Calvin's help he never would have found someone who was willing to do *pro bono* legal work. Letters have arrived from Vietnamese inmates (often requesting malas or pictures of the Buddha) that begin, "Calvin Malone is helping me with this letter as I have difficulty writing English." There's a touching letter from a young man who had just received a package of clothing and some funds who writes, "I owe you a big thank you, and I wish I could show my thanks but I truly don't know how. I never received anything such as this before." He didn't know it, but the person who anonymously orchestrated that gift was Calvin; it was just mailed from the Vermont Zen Center. And then there are the cards from Calvin himself with funds enclosed: "as a donation to ease suffering," "to send someone to camp," "a donation to help," and on and on.

One inmate, Shawn Bayer (introduced in the chapter "Shawn" in this book) writes:

> At first, I could hardly understand how Calvin could continue to do all he did for others day after day. Calvin significantly impacted my life through his example and by patiently being there. He taught me a tremendous amount about things both little and big. He taught me about the importance of knowledge; he taught me about compassion and love, and loyalty and friendship and responsibility. These are things guys don't like to talk about in prison, and Calvin taught me that it was okay to do that too.

Another inmate, Adam Prescot, sent this after reading an early draft of Calvin's book:

> Calvin has been such a good friend and helped me get through some hard times. He made me realize so much about myself. In his book, his personality really shines through exactly as I know it. He brings joy and understanding continuously . . .

In one of the most striking stories, "Soup," the transformation of the person Calvin describes encountering was so remarkable that I asked Calvin to send me some "supporting evidence." Before long, a packet of letters arrived which had been sent to Calvin over the course of several months by Brad (the young man in the story) and by Brad's *mother*. This is what Brad wrote in one of them:

> I was mad at the world, I was angry all the time, and I had no direction. Now I have short-term and long-term goals. I don't use or want to use heavy narcotics. I'm in the best shape of my life physically and spiritually, AND I OWE ALL THIS TO YOU BRO. So if you NEVER help anyone again you can always look back and say you helped a young man that most people his whole life said was beyond help. That's got to be worth something. Not to mention I got my G.E.D!

And this from his mother: "Your ray of light and words touched a place inside Brad I was unable to reach! He thinks the world of you. Thank you!"

Strange things happen in prison. Some people sink to the depths of hell, but others, like Calvin, find in prison the crucible that enables them to make a complete transformation. The result is spiritual growth and the flowering of compassion. Calvin's Buddhist practice has made him look intently at his thoughts, his emotions, his actions, and his reactions.

Whether we are in prison or not, there is not much difference between us; it is more a matter of difference in degree than kind. Any of our thoughts can erupt into emotions; any of our emotions can ignite into actions. For most of us, those actions won't physically place anyone in life-threatening danger. Nevertheless, from the point of view of Buddhism, any time we give way to our baser emotions we do place our life—our life of oneness—in jeopardy.

Although Calvin is not a Zen teacher, he is someone who takes the Dharma seriously and works mindfully to incorporate it into his actions. This goes directly to the marrow of spiritual training—learning to actualize wisdom and compassion in our daily life. The fruit of that work can be seen between the covers this book. Some of the stories are funny, some harrowing, some poignant. All express the Dharma as a vivid reality in one who is trying to *live* practice, and not simply talk about it. This is true Buddhism.

SUNYANA GRAEF
Vermont Zen Center
Shelburne, Vermont

ACKNOWLEDGMENTS

THERE WERE LITERALLY THOUSANDS OF PEOPLE involved in the making of this book: friends of friends, family members related to characters, teachers, students, admirers, and detractors alike. I can only acknowledge a handful, and if I overlooked anyone close it is not intentional—but I hope you know that you too had a hand in making this book possible. Thank you all:

Judy Patterson • Lama Inge • Dharmachari Aryadakha • Ilsang Jackson • Ken & Visakha Kawasaki • Rowan Conrad • Sunyana Graef • Ti'an Callery • Noah Young • Oswaldo Burgos • Dale Crittenden • Clyde Nipp • Dirk McClinton • Brian Lamb • Roy Queen • James "Padma" Pliley • Jacob Meeks • Josh Hobbs • Taigen Henderson • Brian Moore • Jerald Rapali • Victor Vasquez • Randy Robinson • Harvey Talbert • Viet Ngo • Billy Trick • Hung Truong • Keith Schoening • Marc Malone • Jim Bedard • Scott Kobai Whitney • Eido Frances Carney • Dan Bouton • Eleanor Mussen • Vanja Palmers • Shane Kellberg • Richard Sloderbeck • Henry Hodgman • Minh Thach • Steven Baird • The AHCC Buddhist Prison Group • Jeremy Yeager

INTRODUCTION

"THE ONLY THING you own and the only thing you have is your word. Without it you are just a poor, broke-ass inmate." With slight variations, this is common jailhouse wisdom. Over the years I have tried to adhere to this principle, which I believed was irrefutable. But I don't completely believe it anymore.

There are other things you can have. You can have the courage and the perseverance, as well as the dedication, to practice. You can have the ability to transform your thinking and your actions and become a better person. You can have such deep and rewarding friendships that loneliness is no longer an issue. You can have the power to make positive changes within your environment that have a ripple effect going beyond prison boundaries.

1

I know this to be true. But the fact remains that I am in prison, and every once in a while as I wake up, the stark realization of this fact washes over me. One of my biggest fears of imprisonment is becoming "institutionalized." The everyday, every-moment way in which prison exercises control of time, place, and space makes it easy to fall into complacency and dullness. I lie in bed knowing that I face another day of attrition. Of the three meals served, maybe, just maybe, one will be good enough to eat. The large number of mentally ill incarcerated here will wander aimlessly, their unpredictability a constant source of unease. Arbitrary rules will be applied when I least expect them. Violence is just around the corner. Another day of gray loneliness will accompany every activity.

As I allow this line of thinking to run its course, I eventually become aware of how ridiculous all this self-pity is. I am healthy. I am isolated from street violence, car accidents, and other dangers of life on the streets. I am far removed from wars. I am not starving, and I sleep well. I realize that I have allowed myself to be swallowed by delusion—even if just for a few moments. This delusion is the same that people everywhere are subject to. We impose limitations upon ourselves and create a prison more restrictive and harmful than life behind walls and razor wire.

Meditating before my altar transforms my surroundings into something universal. I feel that I am sitting with millions of beings without the shackles of attachment, aversion, or multitudes of other afflictions. It is there where all hindrances and obstacles are dispelled and peace and freedom reigns. This is the great benefit of practicing Dharma in prison.

At the same time this practice can be a pain in the butt. The pain is not due to excessive sitting in front of an altar. It is the pain that accompanies self-realization and honestly facing personal imperfections.

I began Buddhist practice soon after my incarceration. As each year passed, I could actually see profound changes in my perspective. Despite the environment, or maybe because of it, I became a more compassionate and understanding person. Then, just as I convinced myself that I had a fairly good grasp of the basic teachings of the Buddha, along would come a prisoner or guard acting as a teacher to let me know that I had only just begun.

Like anywhere else, there are countless teachers in prison and endless opportunities to practice. On the outside, if you run into a situation that is unpleasant, you have many options at your disposal. You can face it head-on, or you can get in your car and take a drive. You can try to forget by getting drunk or taking drugs, or you can go for a walk in the woods. You can eat what you want, or you can call a friend.

In prison, there are few avenues of escape. Prison is an in-your-face sort of experience. There are violent people, scam artists, the kind-hearted, the predators, the ignorant, the uneducated, those who are sincere, and those who are lazy. Many have given up on their lives and just wander through the day looking for someone or something to help them get past each boring moment. They dump all their concerns on you or ask for advice hoping you can solve their personal difficulties in short sound bites. I have learned to listen to most people more mindfully and with more understanding, but I do not allow them to use me to do their time for them.

As the years folded away into this new millennium, I

became a bit jaded from the onslaught of the suffering around me. The rise in the number of mentally ill imprisoned added another dimension to the pain and suffering so prevalent among those incarcerated. It is difficult to discern the root cause of why some people are here. Add to that those who are addicted to meth, heroin, or some other drug, and you have an environment that can be demoralizing on multiple levels.

For prisoners new to Buddhist practice, the challenge of dealing with the multi-layered problems of other prisoners may be too difficult to surmount. They might find it easier to succumb to the lure of TV or the next card game. For experienced practitioners, there is a tendency to create a "practice cocoon," to insulate themselves from the more unfortunate. Although this can be a means of self-preservation, it also prevents practitioners from opportunities to deepen their practice by engaging with other prisoners who need help and are open to receiving it.

This book has come out of my experiences in prison and is devoted to bringing Buddhist perspectives to those who are interested in making their lives better, in prison or out. Prison can be a hard place—so can the world outside prison gates. If we want to ease each other's suffering, we need to learn how to be compassionate to everyone around us—our friends as well as people who might wish us harm.

In my experience, the Dharma path is a way to achieve true happiness. To follow it fully may be the most difficult challenge of anyone's life. Yet the benefits of doing so are beyond calculation. The kindness we extend to others ripples out into the universe endlessly.

May all beings be happy.
May all beings be well.
May all beings find peace.

RAZOR-WIRE
DHARMA

ENTERING THE WAY

GETTING A JOB in the penitentiary is difficult at best. Most positions are kitchen or janitorial and frequently involve "make-work" chores, like sweeping up cigarette butts or wiping already clean tables. A few inmates are lucky enough to get premium jobs in the education department or in recreation or the library. Vacancies occur if someone dies or goes to "the Hole," and mostly these positions are taken by lifers. Everyone else is relegated to grunt work, especially newcomers.

Three months into my sentence I heard of a job opening in the prison chapel and jumped at the chance, even though I didn't believe I had, as it were, a prayer. The biggest problem facing me at the job interview was the unwritten policy that the Chaplain hired only Christians. I was a devout

9

atheist—a small obstacle that I mulled over and over without resolution right up to the moment of the interview. One of my strengths is being able to do well during interviews. Usually if I get that far, I get the job.

For a long minute the Chaplain and I stared at each other over a large polished wood desk. He was dressed casually and looked relaxed. His glasses were way ahead of their time and distracted me to the point that when he finally spoke it caught me off guard. He asked about my clerical abilities and my level of education. He asked me what I did for a living before prison (I was a warehouse supervisor) and if I had been in the military (I'd been in the army for about three years). All easy questions.

Finally, at the end of the interview, the Chaplain popped the question: "Are you a Christian?"

The brain is kind of funny sometimes. Time stops in certain instances and you feel you have all the time in the world to think of answers. At least I did then. I did not want to grovel and beg for this job. I did not want to lie and say I was Christian. If I did, I'd be going against my own principles. But if I were honest, I knew that there would be no job for me. I blinked a couple of times and without thinking said, "I was baptized Presbyterian." A technically honest answer. The Chaplain beamed at me, enthusiastically slapped the top of the desk with his hand, and said I had the job. We shook hands on it, and so began my first prison job.

Although my duties were mostly clerical, part of them was trying to make sense of the thousands of religious books in the library. The chapel library was tiny with roughly the same floor-space as a city bus. The Chaplain did not believe in the Dewey Decimal System. Organizationally, it was a mess. I never found out what the Chaplain had against Melvil Dewey. Sometimes I entertained the notion that perhaps Dewey never let anyone know if he was baptized Presbyterian or not. Without using Dewey's system, the next best option was to catalog all the books alphabetically.

I soon discovered that all but around one percent of the books were Christian—and basically all of those were some version of Protestant or Fundamentalist. A handful of Jewish books were segregated and partially hidden at the bottom of a corner shelf. Catholic books in Spanish and English had a shelf above that. Mormon, Wiccan, Jehovah's Witness, and Islamic books were kept in wooden boxes or locked in cabinets. If anyone wanted to read those books they had to go through the Chaplain. Few did. When books are locked out of sight, with obstacles hindering access, no one bothers.

IT WAS A DAY LIKE ANY OTHER—isn't it always that way when a life-altering event shakes our complacent lives? It was a Monday morning and I passed through the various check-points between the cellblock and work without any of the usual hassles. On my desk, a load of work had piled up. I went over the "New Arrivals" list then typed a couple of religious event notices. Next I tackled the stack of literature that pours into the prison chapel every day. The library was open for general use, but only three people were taking advantage of the time allocated to them for that purpose. Two of the men I recognized as lifers and daily regulars with nothing else to do. The other was a New Guy. He looked to be in his early twenties and had not yet absorbed that prison mentality—which makes you look and eventually act the part of prisoner. I could tell in an instant that he was a Rookie. Whenever people passed behind him, he ignored them. An old-timer or an experienced convict would shift slightly sideways, without thinking, to be able to see if the person going by posed a threat. This New Guy acted like he was at a bookstore in a mall.

"Excuse me," interrupted my work. There he was, the New Guy, looking all innocent and sincere. I couldn't help thinking that this guy was going to see some dark days once some of the convicts got a good look at him. He was handsome not only by prison standards, but in that countrified, clean-cut, happy-go-lucky way that inexplicably pisses off people who are doing serious prison time. In spite of the surroundings, he carried a youthful optimistic exuberance that penetrated my unfriendly facade. His grin was contagious. I smiled, despite myself, as I responded, "You're excused." Without reacting to my snide manner, he asked if we carried any Buddhist books. His request was so sincere and so politely framed that I replied in kind and apologized for not having any at all.

This was the moment my life was about to change forever.

In one of the locked cabinets there was a meager collection of literature under the classification of "Eastern Religion." Almost all Eastern religions were represented in one way or another, though there was nothing on Buddhism. The next time Norman (as I learned the New Guy was called) returned to the library I showed him the ten or twelve books hoping he would find something of interest. He looked over the collection for more than an hour. Just before he left, he asked if it would be possible to have books sent in.

I asked the Assistant Chaplain if this were a possibility. Of the two Chaplains this one was the most open to religions other than his own. He suggested that we write to Buddhist organizations or publishers to ask for used books. The Chaplain warned us not to expect too much because other religious groups in the prison had tried the same thing with virtually no success. Regardless of this gloomy forecast, we scheduled a time when we could get together to write a "begging letter."

Norman was so persistent about this Buddhist business that my curiosity was aroused. I started digging through dusty boxes filled with discarded literature stacked up in an unused broom closet. As if by magic I found three old copies of *Tricycle* magazine. These I offered to Norman, who in turn gave me one to read. I didn't bother. Partly, I dislike people shoving religious books at me and, frankly, what I did glance at was not that interesting to me.

Several days later Norman showed up again. I was beginning to have mixed feelings about this guy who was obviously smart, yet was starting to be a pest with his questions about getting Buddhist material. He had an engaging personality, but this was dimmed by airs I imagined him to be putting on. I was further irritated when Norman came to the planning meeting carrying two books someone had sent him. One of these he handed to me and flat out told me to look it over. Meanwhile, there was a begging letter to write.

The book Norman gave me was *Mindfulness in Plain English*. In my cell I examined the cover and noticed that it was from Wisdom Publications. I thought that the name of the publisher was a bit presumptuous, and with that skeptical mindset I started reading.

By the time I got through Chapter One I was hooked! Everything I read made complete sense. Here was a path that was inviting me to search for truth without requiring blind trust. I felt that I was being invited to seek a way out of ignorance. Here was something that, without requiring belief, offered me the opportunity to see and practice. Everything I read in this book seemed to encourage me to take logical steps toward real peace and happiness.

When I finished reading the book, I sought out Norman in the prison yard. I wanted to talk to him about this new universe I had discovered. Much to my dismay, Norman was in the weight-lifting area surrounded by four convicts known for their racist views. They were Skinheads connected with the Klan and Aryan Nations groups within the prison. I was extremely concerned for his safety, but had no choice other than to let it go for the time being.

Later, the Assistant Chaplain, Norman, and I got together to discuss the "begging letter" I had written during the course of the week. Again the Chaplain warned us not to expect too much, but he was still willing to let us try. We gleaned over two hundred addresses from the last pages of the *Tricycle* magazines. These addresses included Buddhist temples, centers, various sanghas (Buddhist communities), publishers, Buddhist stores and organizations. The Chaplain offered to mail the letters and pay for postage and supplies with chapel funds. We spent hours addressing and stuffing envelopes. The first sixty letters were mailed that day and over 180 more during the following two weeks.

By then I'd discovered that Norman was exceptionally smart. He let me know that his IQ was hovering at 160. He also let me know that he was gay. Norman took pains to assure me that he was not trying to find a mate in prison. He said that women don't go around having sex with anyone just because they are women and neither do gay people. These revelations didn't seem significant to me—I wanted to talk with him about Buddhism, being in the present, and mindfulness. I wanted to know what you do when meditating, or better yet, I wanted to learn techniques. We agreed to meet in the yard that weekend.

The day we walked the yard I learned a bit more about Norman and Buddhism. Norman was raised in a communal environment, a lifestyle that reflected the peace and love ideals of the '60s. We talked about a lot of things that day, though all I remember was his trying to convince me that living in the present was most important. I simply could not, did not, want to get it. I countered his explanations with questions concerning planning for the future. If you live for the moment and forget the past your future will be riddled with the same mistakes over and over. If you do not plan ahead, you plan to fail. That was my perspective. Norman patiently tried to help me understand that this is the only time there is. He said, "Yesterday is history, tomorrow a mystery, and the moment is a gift. That's why they call it the present."

I think now that most of my resistance to what he had to say stemmed from my resentment at having this youngster try to teach me something (after all, he was twenty-two years my junior). We argued a bit, sometimes adamantly, but not so much as to make me unaware of the many eyes watching us walk the track. I felt the presence of looming danger—the same sort of feeling one gets when dark, threatening clouds mass on the horizon and the wind changes, growing steadily. There was electricity in the air. I could almost smell the ozone. *Something wicked this way comes . . .*

NORMAN HAD GOTTEN PERMISSION from the Chaplain to meditate in one of the side rooms of the chapel. I wasn't interested in sitting there doing nothing and didn't join him. But a Vietnamese inmate did. Everyone called him Lanh. He was a quiet, gentle person who got along with Norman from the start. In fact, Norman began speaking in Vietnamese with Lanh. Norman would do the same with Spanish-speaking people as well; I figured that he was a natural linguist. Norman constantly amazed me. There he was sitting on the bare floor, a slight smile on his face, next to another young man from another country, both looking serene.

In the chapel office, I went to work looking over the new arrival list and then began sorting the chapel mail. There in the pile of letters and packages were two letters and four boxes addressed to the Prison Buddhist Group. The Chaplain opened the packages and handed them over to me. They were filled with Buddhist books! All kinds of Buddhist books! Someone included a box of incense and colorful postcards of various Buddhist statues. One of the letters was from Ilsang Jackson of the Zen Temple in Ann Arbor, Michigan, offering assistance. The other was from Sensei Sunyana Graef of the Vermont Zen Center, letting us know that books were on the way. I am writing to both of these wonderful teachers to this day. That day, I remember, I was overwhelmed by the generosity of those whom I had never met.

When Norman and Lanh finished their session, I showed them the boxes. What a wonderful time we had going over each text, excitedly making plans for the future. Even I was caught up in the moment.

No one has yet devised a form of communication that is faster than word-of-mouth in prison—and the next week seven people showed up for Norman's practice, now called the Buddhist Time. By then, over a dozen boxes had arrived, each full of Dharma books. A miracle had occurred. The letters were pouring in. I began to seriously look at this religion that moved people to such levels of generosity without asking anything in return. I began sitting with the group and started thinking of myself as a Buddhist, albeit at first with certain reservations. Although I had not yet formally taken refuge, I tried to be aware of the suffering around me and how I contributed to that suffering. I felt a deep connection to the Dharma which began to transform the way I thought about nearly everything. Within a month we had thirty people practicing.

The numbers grew every week and donations of books, tapes, and incense arrived daily unabated. In the end it was estimated that $15,000 to $20,000 in new and used books were received by the Buddhist group. From those generous acts of kindness a prison Buddhist Sangha sprang forth and eventually spread to all the prisons in Washington State. But that came later. Events at the time were soon to force me to examine who I was and the direction life was taking me.

PRISON IS A REFLECTION of the society that maintains it, a microcosm of life outside prison walls without the veneer of societal civility—and race is a constant issue. Remove the laws that help maintain equality, remove human rights, destroy hope and nurture despair, and I bet you would find that a surprising number of people outside of prison would behave the way most prisoners do.

Racially divided groups seem to form naturally in prison, mainly to support group members' beliefs and to provide protection against opposing groups. At the time I was getting to know Norman, men in prison lived together according to race. Each race had a section in the chow hall. This was not something imposed upon the inmates by prison officials; it was something the inmates imposed upon themselves. Prison officials, however, do not discourage racial divisions and use it as a controlling mechanism to "divide and conquer."

Unless you were looking for serious trouble, you did not sit simply anywhere to eat. First you had to find a table that would accept you, and it had to be one from your own race. There was a small group of brave men of all races who had a section of tables. These were the very rare exceptions—and this was the group I gravitated toward. I refused to be involved in the daily drama of race hate. The people I associated with were those willing to stand up against heavy pressure and not succumb to the ideals of the masses. Nonetheless, you cannot escape the unpredictable explosions of violence that simmer near the surface of any given day.

Walking in the yard with friends one fine spring afternoon, I was enjoying the feel of the sun after the long winter cold. We were all just kicking it, talking about nothing important, joking about the bad food, our lives, our plight, making light of our circumstances. I was struck by the diversity of the group: a Mexican, an Asian, two whites, two blacks—just being. I expanded my gaze to take in the rest of the yard. A large group of Mexicans was playing soccer. A group of Native Americans passed by us. But suddenly I realized that there was something amiss. At first I thought it was the lack of blacks that had caught my attention until I remembered that there was a basketball tournament going on in the gym, which was far removed from the yard. Still, a feeling of unease was settling down around me.

Moments before it happened I became aware of the unusual number of "Bikers" and racists gathering all along the wall containing the telephones. There were scores of men lined up half the length of a football field. In the time it takes to snap a finger, a cry arose and shouts grew to a crescendo until the unified shout of "White Power" could be distinctly heard. Dust obscured the scene as yells and cries of fear broke through this chant of hate and misguided pride.

My friends and I were on the farthest corner of the track when the incident erupted. As we turned toward the melee, I still did not know what was going on or why, when out of the dust burst a young, skinny guy. The splatters of blood contrasted with his T-shirt as much as his black skin did. He cut to the right but there was no escape or help in that direction and he immediately changed course. Zigzagging through the crowd, he desperately looked in every direction seeking to escape an unseen assailant. Close behind him, emerging from the thick dust like an aberration out of a B-rated movie were three large men in pursuit. The one with waist-length hair and his heavy-set partner soon gave up the chase, disappearing back into the dust cloud and the men massed along the wall.

A kaleidoscopic view of the scene seemed to rush into my mind in broken segments. I noticed that there were fewer than ten blacks in the entire yard. Only for a split second did I wonder what had precipitated this. I prayed that the youngster would not run in my direction as I saw him head toward the weight-lifting area. His pursuers were gaining on him and he seemed to know it. The frightened inmate abruptly cut to the right and ran toward me.

Suddenly, and instinctively, my perspective changed. I became calculating, reacting out of self-preservation. I knew the two would pass near me within seconds. I refused to run knowing that I could become the target anyway—any sign of weakness would turn the mob's rage in my direction. The only thing I could do was face the violence. The blood on the T-shirt held my attention until I looked into the young man's eyes. They were wide with fear and resignation. Steps before he got to me, he turned sharply to his left. Caught off guard by the maneuver, the man chasing him continued running toward me. He was yelling, "Come here, nigger." His eyes were wild and his momentum was carrying him to me.

I began walking calmly in his direction talking loud enough to be heard. "I remember you," I said, forcing my face into a smile to throw off the assailant's confidence. "We played volleyball the other day and you know what? You're not that athletic. In fact you aren't all that tough." The knife in his hand looked more like an ice-pick, but I could clearly see the blood on it. I showed my teeth in a big smile. "Come here," I invited him real friendly-like. He stopped with a confused look on his face as if waking from a trance. I was not going to let him be the aggressor as I kept up my mindless chatter and moved closer. One of my friends tried to grab my shirt but I pulled away still talking. "Oh, come here baby, I'm not some youngster like the one you stuck. I got something for you." He faltered as I came closer still.

In this explosive situation, I could see several things going on at the same time. Two blacks had reached the weight area and now brandished steel weight bars keeping the mass of racists at bay. As long as they controlled that area, the chances that the rest of us would be beaten to death were greatly diminished. I also noticed that guards were forming all along the wall above us and around the guard towers. I took another step forward, coming just feet from having to do something other than talk, when a guard began firing his weapon. Instantly men began scattering. The yard doors on my left opened and guards poured in by the dozens. The man with the shank turned and ran. Now three blacks had weight bars and one was attacking the group of whites being pushed by the guards. Shots were going off as dust and dried grass swirled. My friends and I moved further away from the center of the action and deeper into the corner of the yard.

Guards on the wall pointed to individuals so that officers on the ground could cuff up all those involved in the riot. I thought I would be hauled off as well but we were ignored in our corner. At five o'clock that evening most of us were still in the yard when they began processing us out nine at a time. We were patted down first, then passed through the yard gate to the open courtyard. There we were made to strip and then be thoroughly searched again. Finally we were sent to our cells and locked down.

Dinner was served at eight that evening and only by tiers. Usually meals are called by prison blocks—one side goes to the chow hall, then the other, 272 men on each side, 68 men on each tier, four tiers high on each side. But this night, they called only one tier to dinner at a time, then they locked the men up and called the next tier of 68. It took several hours before everyone had eaten. Guards were stationed on a catwalk in the chow hall, each carrying a rifle. The one semi-peaceful place you could go to escape the tension was the chapel. I was grateful to have somewhere to stay during the lockdown period as tensions continued to be high.

I didn't see Norman for some time after that, and when I did it was at the practice session. He was not his usual cheery self. Instead, he was withdrawn and quiet. He hardly spoke to me and left immediately after practice, not lingering with the books or socializing as before. I could tell that the ongoing racial tensions frightened him. I know it frightened me.

A COUPLE OF WEEKS after the riot I was finishing lunch in the chow hall when one of the guys at my table got up and Norman sat down. I was startled. Looking around to see who was watching, I turned back to him and noticed that the expression on his face was anxious and desperate. Before I could say anything more than "Hello," he burst into tears. The other two men at the table mumbled they had to go and split. Norman dried his eyes on a paper napkin, apologized, and said he was having serious problems.

He told me that after the riot, several Skinheads approached him and warned him not to hang out with any "mud people." They told him he needed their protection and tried to get him to move into their cells. They were even so bold as to say they wanted him as their "bitch." Norman was shaking as he told me this. I looked over at the Aryan section of the chow hall. No one seemed to be paying attention to us. That was when Norman dropped the bombshell. He said that he knew I had only one cellmate and wanted to know if he could move into my cell.

Due to his fragility, I didn't want to straight out tell him no. Instead, I asked if he had talked with one of the members of the Buddhist group who also had room in his cell.

Norman told me that he already did and was turned down because he is gay. Unable to come up with a viable excuse, I went for the obvious and said that there were no racially mixed cells and there would be a danger to all of us if it happened. Tears began to course down his face and I knew with certainty that he was not only desperate but that I was his last option. I resented his intrusion into my life and could only think, "Welcome to prison, kid."

Looking me straight in the eye, he pleaded with me. "I have three choices, Calvin. I live with the Aryans and be exchanged for sex, I go to Protective Custody where doing time is even more restrictive, or I move in with you." I did not say no. I couldn't. But I did try to weasel out of it by letting him know that this was not solely my decision. My current cellmate, Ted, was also involved in making the decision of who could move in.

Ted was an exceptional man, highly motivated, quiet with a big natural smile made brilliant against a black expressive face. He held multiple black-belt degrees in several forms of martial arts. We got along extremely well, but I was not sure how he would respond to Norman's request for asylum. To get out of the uncomfortable position I was in, I promised Norman that I would ask Ted as soon as possible. He thanked me, then left the chow hall with resignation on his face.

Ted was in the cell when I got there after lunch. I broached the question of Norman moving in. He surprised me with his comment: "Cal, you're the OG"—the Old Guy—"of the house. If you think this is best for him, then it is all right with me." Simple as that. I warned Ted that there could be trouble because some of the prominent Aryans in the prison wanted Norman to move into their cells. Again, Ted matter-of-factly shrugged and asked me if that was my only worry. Thanking him for his input, I went to work.

Norman showed up at the library an hour later. Ignoring me, he went to the Buddhist cabinet that was now overflowing with books. As he seemed absorbed in what he was doing, I waited until after the meditation period before telling him that Ted was not opposed to the idea of having a white guy move in. Norman's face broke out in a smile of relief. He reminded me that I was half white and Ted didn't mind that half. Purposely trying to subdue his feelings of relief and joy, I reminded him that the unit sergeant had to approve the move. I was not too concerned now, because the decision was out of my hands and most likely the move would not be approved.

I was surprised when the sergeant promptly approved the move. Amid cries of disbelief and protest from the occasional cell, Norman carried his belongings down the tier to my cell. What's more, none of us experienced a single problem from anyone about our integrated cell.

Our living arrangement worked out better than expected. Ted and Norman got along well. The two worked out clandestinely in the cell. Displays of martial arts in any form are strictly prohibited, including tai chi. Ted taught both of us this form of art, but it was Norman who soaked it up like a sponge. Our life in the confines of the small cell was as pleasant as you could want or hope for.

SOMETHING WOKE ME UP one night. Something was not right. I lay in the darkness trying to clear the dream fabrics from my mind. The luminous dial on the clock showed me that it was 2:30 in the morning. With a jolt, I knew what was wrong. There was no noise. Usually there is a constant hum of conversation, music, TV, and even occasional shouts that echo throughout the cell-block. The hour seldom makes a difference. Noise is a constant companion in prison. It was the lack of noise that woke me up. The dead quiet scared me. What could have made everyone so quiet? The answer came all too soon. A piercing scream cut through the night, making me jump. This was followed by another and then again. The screams became sobs and I could clearly hear a voice pleading for someone to stop. A desperate call for help, then distinctly I heard, "Oh God." This was followed by more whimpering and crying.

It was Geoff. I had met him at the holding facility in Shelton a year earlier. We happened to eat together and got to know each other in the same way strangers do when they meet on a long bus or train ride. He was a scared youngster who tried to act as though he had a handle on life. I liked him well enough to talk to him, but forgot about him as soon as I was sent to Walla Walla.

After Norman had moved in with Ted and me, Geoff showed up at the institution. I spoke with him and tried to relay as much information about the place as I could. Unfortunately, within three days of his arrival the Aryans got hold of him. They filled his head with dire warnings of danger allegedly coming from blacks and Hispanics. They offered him protection and a place to "belong." They scared him so much that he stopped talking to me and began to hang around "the Fellas." Then I heard that he was being offered a cell to live in on my tier and only three gates down. That cell housed Big Phil, notorious for sexually and physically assaulting the vulnerable. I was in a dilemma. If I pulled Geoff aside and tried to dissuade him from moving there, I would have put myself in grave danger. Then the comfortable existence I had worked so carefully to create would be shattered. I made all kinds of excuses to myself and did nothing. Now I was hearing the result. Phil was raping Geoff.

As I lay there, I could feel sweat popping up on my forehead. My heart pounded so loudly I could hear it. I looked over to the double bunks next to me. The light coming into the cell from outside the bars made it easy to see that both Ted and Norman were awake, both lying on their backs, both staring upward. We could hear Geoff call out again and again then slowly quiet down to muffled sounds. Norman's voice cut into the dark, "That could have been me," he said. I could tell he was crying.

Lying there I felt like a coward. I admonished myself for not intervening when I had the chance. Right then and there I changed. At once I saw all the mean, evil, unkind things I had ever done. It was overpowering. Even memories of kicking over ant piles came to mind. I thought of the numerous ways I had caused others to suffer. I was not the mostly nice guy I thought I was. That realization broke my heart.

Seeing myself without the illusory trappings created by pride, ignorance, and selfishness was painful, and what I saw was repugnant to me. Shock is not an adequate word to describe my reaction. I felt despair at the knowledge that much of what I believed was flawed. Shame overwhelmed me as I turned over, face down on my pillow. I cried uncontrollably.

When the guards opened the cells for breakfast that next morning, I moved hastily out and down the tier. Geoff walked out as I got to his cell. There were marks on his neck and a slight bruise under his jaw. Phil was asleep as we walked along the tier. I asked him if he was okay. He looked down and nodded and shuffled away from me. I vowed right then that I would do everything I could to no longer be a source of suffering. I vowed to always intervene no matter the danger to me. I vowed to do what I could to help those in need. Sometimes I fail—and can only try over and over again to avoid being the source of further suffering.

Now I try to take it one step further and be the source of hope and happiness for those who are too weak with sorrow to find joy in this life. In the process I, too, find happiness.

IN TIME, Norman was transferred to a better prison. I felt his departure keenly. In the time we were together I had learned a lot more than I ever expected. I was meditating and following a whole new path. My view had changed as I looked at the world through different eyes. The qualities instilled in me as a youth growing up in post–World War II Germany, surrounded by bombed-out buildings and people too war-weary to be unkind, acted as fertile ground for Norman to plant the seeds of compassion.

Norman got out of prison a while ago and asked me to call him. We talked as if no time had passed. We talked as only best friends can talk. He was working at a good job earning an excellent salary. He was happy and he thanked me for helping him survive his prison sentence. I miss him terribly at times. It was tough to say goodbye to my first teacher.

THE ABYSS

MY FATHER, the grandson of a former slave, was born into a large, poor family in rural South Carolina. My mother was born in Munich to a family surrounded by comfort and culture. During World War II, my mother's family was virtually wiped out, along with all of their possessions. My father had enlisted toward the end of the war, and it was during that time that my parents met and married.

My brother Marc and I were born in Munich. While I received a lot of attention in post-War Germany, my brother always seemed to lag behind. Throughout our years together in school, Marc was always known as "Cal's little brother." When our family arrived in America for the first time, it was difficult for our biracial, German-speaking family to adjust to the social differences and racial attitudes of a country heralded as a land of opportunity and freedom.

To further complicate matters, we had a language barrier at home. My father spoke only English. My brother and I spoke only German. My mother spoke French, German, and English. Simple events like dinner often turned into a major production that left my mother exhausted. At one memorable dinner, as we sat down to eat, my father asked how everyone's day had been. I asked my mother what my father had just said. She told me that he had asked how our day was. My father then asked what it was that I said. My mother told him that I had inquired about his inquiry. When that was all settled, I asked my father to pass the mashed potatoes. He asked my mother to translate what I had just said. She told him, and we would be off on another linguistic tango. In short order I was able to understand English, but had problems formulating correct sentences. More often than not it was extremely difficult to make myself understood.

One day a neighbor came to visit and brought a bag of marshmallows. She told me they were delicious and that all American children loved them. Well, I was not going to be any different than American children, so I enthusiastically stuck one of the huge spongy things into my mouth. Now, most likely you were brought up on marshmallows, and you're used to the taste and texture. I would even venture to guess that the feel and flavor of a marshmallow brings back fond childhood memories. I had no such advantage.

This thing in my mouth was *horrible*. The neighbor, confusing my look of terror for unadulterated delight, offered me a bowl full of those nasty monsters.

As soon as no one was looking I took the soggy, abhorrent material from my mouth. Not wanting to disappoint this kind woman, but desperate to do something with the offending confection, I chucked it under the couch. My plan was to get rid of all of the marshmallows in this manner and later, when no one was around, gather the discarded squishy things from beneath the couch and throw them away.

The neighbor asked me how I liked the marshmallow. In my broken English I told her that I had never tasted anything like them before. This made her very happy and every week she brought over a gigantic bag to help smooth my transition into American society. Unfortunately, I forgot about the marshmallows accumulating under the couch. I really meant to retrieve those things and trash them. My mother discovered the mass of white stuff when she noticed that ants were attempting to walk off with our couch.

SCHOOL WAS ANOTHER WORLD ALTOGETHER. For me it was a place to observe other children. The boys in my class never talked or played with me, and whenever I did say a rare word or two the reaction was uncontrolled laughter. I was glad to make everyone happy. If I saw someone who looked sad I would start talking with him. It always caused a reaction; at least they weren't sad anymore. Several children had nicknames, and they gave me one too—that's when I knew I was in. The children in my school were finally getting used to me. They would point at me and laugh, I'd wave back and smile, and that would make them laugh more.

At home, my father asked me if I was getting along better at school. I assured him that all was absolutely perfect and that I was becoming popular because the kids gave me a new nickname. My father asked me what my new name was as he took a bite of cake. I told him that the children called me "Nigger"—at which my father choked and cake went everywhere. I told him that milk helps when eating cake.

AS WE GOT OLDER, my brother Marc found it impossible to connect with anyone or anything. I tried to encourage him to get involved in the things I liked, but aside from being in the California redwoods, he never enjoyed the outdoors the way I did. The few activities he tried to engage in didn't appeal to him, and he was never accepted by others. Being of mixed race, we experienced tremendous pressure. Each of us dealt with it differently. My younger sister Joan had problems which at times were severe, but she managed to overcome them and carve out a happy life for herself. I blissfully waded through life like the emperor without clothes, not knowing I was different until someone told me. Marc internalized everything, becoming withdrawn and quiet.

Like many young people who are unable to find acceptance among their peers, Marc found companionship with drugs and alcohol. Being high gave Marc the feeling of comfort and acceptance that everyone craves and provided him with an illusion of contentment. But it never lasted long. It took greater and greater amounts of drugs and alcohol to dull his senses. All they really did was put his problems and stress on hold until sober moments of glaring reality confronted him.

Looking back on it now, I can think of a hundred things my family or society or I could have done for Marc. At the time, none of us foresaw where his addiction would ultimately lead. Like millions of people who have loved ones addicted to drugs and alcohol, we felt helpless and hoped that it was just a passing phase.

AFTER HIGH SCHOOL I joined the army and went over-seas. Toward the end of my tour of duty my brother joined the army. He was dismissed before I was discharged. His drug abuse had gotten so bad that even the army, rife with drug and alcohol problems in its ranks, could not tolerate it anymore.

When I left the service and saw my brother, I was shocked. He seemed older than his years and even more entrenched in his abusive patterns. My family tried to be supportive, but in the long run that support enabled him to sink further into his drug addiction. My parents were divorced by this time. Marc would stay with one or the other until he wore out his welcome. The only joy in his life was getting high. There seemed to be no way out. My brother was determined to sink further down into the abyss of drug-induced despair.

I, too, was having serious problems. I had become addicted to drugs and alcohol while in the military. Although I managed to get an honorable discharge, the chemical dependency of heroin addiction and alcoholism made my successes short-lived and my anger explosive. It destroyed my life. I verbally and physically assaulted and abused all those who cared about me. I sought refuge in the feelings I had as a child and tried to grasp the illusion of perfection I remembered. I became self-absorbed in my quest for that magical happiness. Nothing helped. I felt myself becoming harder, turning to stone. In the process, I hurt many people and drove myself from the prison I created to the cinderblock and razor-wire one I am in now.

AFTER MY FIRST YEAR IN PRISON, I earned the privilege of an EFV or an Extended Family Visit. These visits differ from conventional visits because the prisoner can have their immediate family stay overnight with them in specially built apartments. It is one of the few times a prisoner is not under the eye of a guard, camera, or some other monitor. It provides the opportunity for family to get together privately and enjoy each other's company, sharing home-cooked meals devoid of any prison flavors.

When I learned that I had been approved for the EFV, I immediately called my mother to give her the news and set up a date. Throughout our conversation, my mother sounded unusually breathless and bursting with enthusiasm. While I could appreciate the excitement surrounding the pending visit, her response seemed somehow out of proportion. I finally asked her what was going on. She said that she had some wonderful news and would share it when she saw me during the EFV. I tried to pry it out of her, but she would not budge. It made me smile to hear her sound so happy. A dozen possibilities ran through my mind, but nothing seemed to fit. I had to wait a couple of months before I would find out.

The visit was our first since I had gone to prison, and it was both joyful and stressful. It was wonderful to see my mother again, but having to go through the invasive strip-search and intrusive scrutiny prior to the visit made it difficult to get in the mood to socialize in a non-prison environment.

We talked about family news and about my personal possessions that needed to be sold or stored. We prepared a meal together and chatted about everything and about nothing, but she never brought up the "exciting news."

In the evening, I broke down and begged her to tell me. Smiling widely, my mother told me she was buying a house. For our family this was huge. We had lived in several locations on the Monterey Peninsula and in Europe, because the army reassigned my father to a new place every three or four years. We lived in military installations or we rented. We never could afford to buy a home anyway. I was thrilled and very surprised at this unexpected news.

My mother told me that she had seen an ad in the newspaper about a community being built on the Oregon coast, and she inquired about it. Brochures were sent and a sales representative visited to explain the details. After contemplating it, my mother felt that the cost was more than she could handle. Pat, the man handling the sales of the properties, tried to help her find a deal within her means. He suggested that she buy the first home built and allow the agency to use that home as an office and as a model until all the homes were sold. In exchange, my mother would buy the home at a reduced rate and a small patch of land would be included at no cost. My mother felt this was more than fair and decided to look into the company building the community.

Contacting state officials in Salem, Oregon, she learned that a community-housing permit had been granted and that construction was underway to lay in roads, water, and power. She also found that those involved were bonded. She called Pat at his office and asked if she could see the property.

Arrangements were made, and they drove together to the location outside Lincoln City. There, along a hillside in view of a lake and the coastal mountain range, trucks and bulldozers crawled up and down the construction site. In other spots men surveyed and measured. Lots had already been marked off and paved roads laid to most of the sites.

Pat told my mother that if she wanted to accept the deal she could pick out her lot now and they would go back to Portland to write up the contract. My mother walked around the site, climbing the hill and looking around. She came to a lot that had a large pine tree on it and a great view of the lake. This was it! Pat smiled at her choice and went to talk with a group of men working nearby, pointing to my mother and the little property on the hill.

Back in Portland, Pat met with my mother and a representative from her bank. Together they went over the contract. My mother would pay down about a third of the cost. Another third was due upon completion of her house. The remainder was to be financed at a reasonable monthly rate my mother felt she could handle on her fixed income. The down payments were going to come from an inheritance she received from her aunt in Lohr, Germany.

Just before visiting me in September for the EFV, my mother had paid the first deposit and approved the floor plan for a three-bedroom home. It was well suited for our family, though modest by most standards, and the lot was large enough for a garden.

At the EFV my mother happily told me that she now had a place for Marc to live and there was room for me when I got out of prison. At last there seemed to be a home for our family.

Marc arrived from Indiana to help my mother prepare for the move. There was a lot to do. The rapid rate at which the house was being built meant that it would be completed by late winter.

IN THE FALL, an officer came by my cell and told me that I needed to call home. As soon as I got through, my mother, in a very solemn voice, told me that Pat had swindled her and that the whole thing had been a big rip off.

Just before Thanksgiving, my mother had tried to contact Pat about the second payment. He could not be found. All attempts to locate him at his office and through his answering service failed. Desperate, my mother had managed to contact the contractors building the community. They had never heard of Pat. Further investigation revealed that Pat had printed up fake brochures and business cards. He had set up a dummy office and an elaborate scam using existing building sites and falsifying records as well as certifications. He had done this not only to my mother, but to nearly two dozen other individuals and couples.

On the phone, my mother broke down and cried uncontrollably. There was nothing I could do. I felt helpless. I felt at fault somehow. *If only I had not gone to prison.*

Marc did what he could, but after several weeks, as state officials, the police, and other agencies became involved, he thought it would be best if he returned to Indiana. He did not want to be a further financial burden on our mother.

ON DECEMBER 18, 1994, when I went to work at the prison chapel, the Chaplain called me into his office and asked if I had a brother named Marc. I told him I did. The

Chaplain then told me that Marc had died. A newspaper boy had found him early in the morning frozen to death between two houses. A shocked numbness went through me. My father had died of causes related to Agent Orange while I was incarcerated, and now my brother Marc was gone. But his death was different from my father's—it was directly the fault of a specific individual: Pat. At least that was how I viewed it then.

I could feel a lump of hatred beginning to grow deep inside me, like burning coal. The hatred I felt intensified and grew hotter. I had been a practicing Buddhist for about sixteen months at that time. Our sangha did not have a teacher but I practiced every day in my cell and with the group every week. I had read many teachings and thought of myself as being on the road to understanding and compassion. It all disappeared. Though I kept up my practice, the coal-fire hatred smoldered on.

Throughout 1995 that red-hot coal of hate burned in me. Pat eventually got caught in California and was sent to a Federal Prison in Oregon. He received a sentence of about seven years. I was glad that it wasn't a longer sentence, not because I was compassionate, but because a plan was developing in my mind: I would make Pat suffer. Years after he got out of prison, I too would one day be released. Pat would have no reason to think anyone would be coming after him. He would be easy to find and just as easy to get.

I thought of a dozen terrible things I could do to him. None were good enough. After I was transferred to the Airway Heights Correction Center, a plan solidified. I would get out and learn everything I could about him: where he ate, what he did, who he did it with, where he lived. I would learn his patterns. Instead of killing him I planned to shoot him in the leg one night when he left home on some errand. I figured that an arrow dipped in shit would do the most damage. If he survived, I would do it again a year or so later. If he lived, he would always fear the dark and the unknown. That fear, along with a little help from me, would be enough to drive him mad. I went over and over each detail, changing one thing or another and refining every point. I had the time to make it foolproof.

MY HATE WAS FUELED by my feelings of guilt for not having done more for my brother and for being in prison. I felt that I had let my mother down, and I had let my brother down. I justified my vengeful thinking, even in the midst of my Buddhist practice, by convincing myself that I had not played out this retaliation and therefore had done no harm. And so, the fire burned on. But the thing about fires is that they need oxygen and more fuel to continue burning.

I don't know exactly what it was that made me change my thinking. I just know when it happened. I believe now that it had a lot to do with the struggle to maintain a balance between the loving-kindness and understanding that Buddhists outside of prison were showing me and the very real hatred that I had cultivated. My Buddhist practice was making it harder to maintain the anger that stoked the flames of my evil plan. Each month the struggle became more difficult. Soon the struggle became bigger than the hate.

I wrote to my friend in Switzerland, Zen Priest Vanja Palmers, and told him how I felt. He was far enough away from this prison for me to feel safe to reveal my dark intentions. Without judgment, and with complete understanding, Vanja simply said:

> These emotions, ideas, and thoughts become powerful and real only when you become attached to them. When you are attentive to the moment at hand, that is when all those other things disappear. Your freedom and happiness will be determined by your ability to forgive and your ability to express loving-kindness through every deed and thought. To forgive yourself is perhaps the first step. Be good to yourself.

That letter, for some reason, cut through my self-indulgent hate and made me sit up and see that I could not be Pat's karma. Vanja made it clear that Pat had provided me with an important opportunity to further deepen my practice. That moment of clarity was a shock to me, and one of immense relief. I no longer had to carry the heavy burden of hate and anger. This transformation was not, of course, complete and final. It goes on to this day, allowing me to dwell in all possibilities. I still have moments of anger and dislike. Often they dissolve as quickly as they appear.

I know, though, that Vanja's words would not have taken root within me had I not been the beneficiary of letters and teachings from a dozen other sources long before that. Buddhists from all over the U.S. and Canada had in little ways influenced my thinking. Their letters and genuine concern were like jewels shining through my mud of confusion.

It is with gratefulness that I now have plans other than my vengeful machinations: one day I hope to go to the redwoods that Marc enjoyed before his illness and just sit with him in memory.

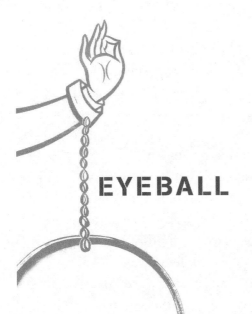

EYEBALL

IN PRISON you do not stare at another prisoner unless you are looking for trouble. To "eyeball" someone is to loudly proclaim that you are a bad-ass and challenge him to dispute it. It's an alpha-male, testosterone thing that runs rampant whenever a large number of men are contained in a small space with little to do and not much to hope for. And to not stare back when being stared at is tantamount to a show of submission.

I was finishing lunch one day when I looked up and saw another prisoner staring in my direction from across several tables. I looked down at what was left of my food hoping that he was not looking at me. A few minutes later I took another glance and, yes, there he was, *looking at me*! My battle instincts kicked in and without thought or hesitation I stared back.

The rest of the men at his table were Skinheads, and possibly members of the KKK. The next thing that struck me was his appearance. He was hunched over his food tray as if protecting it like a dog guarding raw steak. His head was shaved and oddly shaped like a poorly inflated soccer ball that had been kicked around too much. When he talked his lower lip became pointed and reptilian. There was nothing nice about the way this man looked or about the way he was looking at me. Fortunately, he got up with his friends and left the dining hall glancing back in my direction frequently. I never encountered him again while in Walla Walla, but two years later, after being transferred to the Airway Heights Correction Center, newly built for those, like me, who had lower custody levels (custody level is the degree of supervision required for each offender: minimum, medium, close, and "administrative segregation"), I got a close-up of the man when I visited the well-stocked library for the first time.

Harold worked at the checkout counter and looked even crazier and meaner than I remembered. He now sported a Mohawk haircut that accentuated his lumpy head. When I went to check out some books his eyes followed me like a lion looking at a wounded gazelle. I was nervous, but tried to act nonchalant. As it turned out, I would get a job working in the library a week later.

Over the next year, I had to work closely with Harold. I was chagrined to find that my preconceptions about him were, in fact, all wrong. He was considerate and helpful, and under that rough exterior was a pleasant person to talk to. Before long, we became good friends.

He told me that for a long time he had been a bitter, mean, violent, and deeply troubled man. After his incarceration in the mid-1980s, he escaped from prison. The officers who finally caught him, thinking he was armed and dangerous, shot him several times, once in the stomach. He was severely wounded and almost died. That was how he ended up at the maximum-security prison in Walla Walla.

While Harold was in Walla Walla, he fell in with the Aryans and spent most of his time lifting weights. At Airway Heights that kind of prison activity couldn't satisfy Harold, and, out of the blue, he asked me about Buddhism. I invited him to attend our practice—and that was all it took. Harold dedicated himself to Buddhism. He did a lot of work to help build the Sangha and brought in new members who might never have joined. After becoming a Buddhist, Harold settled down to such a degree that none of his old friends recognized him.

A few years ago, Harold was transferred yet again to another prison. He is credited with helping establish a Buddhist practice at his new location and is a role-model to all those lucky enough to meet him.

THANKS TO HAROLD, I don't attach as much importance to appearances or first encounters as I used to.

BANANA

IN EACH OF US there is an old acquaintance, our garrulous ego, clamoring for attention, trying to distract us from what we should see. Ego is a trickster, always calculating ways to prevent you from being aware. When we allow ego to reign supreme, we miss the beauty in each moment.

Someone once told me that while giving a talk at the Maryland Correctional Institution, Thich Nhat Hanh said, "Mindfulness is a kind of energy that helps us be aware of what is going on. Being mindful in everything we do throughout the day, be it drinking or walking, eating or going to the bathroom, brings solidity, freedom, and dignity."

Awareness is a side-effect of practice that enables us to see life more clearly and not let it pass by. The less we focus on "self," the easier it is to see what would normally be missed.

By being more aware, we can help alleviate suffering and better identify those special moments that change our lives.

One the other hand, the potential consequences of a lack of awareness became chillingly apparent to me some months after I met Ben.

BEN WAS THE KIND OF PRISONER who makes an old timer cringe. A classic case of Dennis-the-Menace syndrome, he was an accident waiting to happen. Not only did he look the part but his every movement was a perilous flight toward disaster. You could blame his actions on youthful exuberance or just plain idiocy. Either way, Ben knew how to get into trouble. This made him a perfect target for inmates who could not stand people who weren't following the demeanor and code of "the convict." Ben didn't walk the walk or talk the talk. Other prisoners couldn't deal with his spontaneous bursts of laughter and his ready sense of humor, and the beat of the drummer Ben listened to was not one most others could discern.

Unfortunately for Ben, he was often in over his head before he realized it. He was one of those people who simply did not adapt to prison life. He never meant harm and hardly spoke a mean word and yet this somehow brought him in conflict with fellow inmates.

My first contact with him was during mail-line. Ben was in front of me, laughing and talking with people in line as if he were at the beach. When he got to the front of the line, he was handed an envelope that had been rejected by the prison mailroom. He stood there, looking perplexed, trying to figure out why his letter didn't go out. I understood his predicament. Prison rules can be capricious and applied arbitrarily.

Incoming and outgoing mail is rejected frequently for reasons as simple as smelling of perfume, having a smiley sticker, or containing crayon drawings.

Knowing how important contact with outside friends and family is, I introduced myself and told him why his mail had been rejected. Not only did he use the wrong envelope, but he had not filled out the proper form for "indigent postage." If he resubmitted the postage request it would mean that several more days would pass before his letter could be mailed—so I provided him with a few pre-stamped envelopes. He politely thanked me and we went our separate ways.

ONE MORNING, bananas were being served at breakfast. They were not the usual blemished bananas that we normally got—these actually *looked* like bananas! I had to go to work and didn't have time to take my banana back to the living unit. Thinking that it would be nice to have the fruit available after work I looked for someone to take it back for me. No one was there except Ben. He gladly volunteered when I asked him and off to work I went.

That evening I asked him for my banana. He went to his cell and brought out this brownish mass that sort of resembled a banana but looked more like something you would flush away than any fruit I'd ever seen. As innocently as you can imagine he handed this brown mushy object to me, smiling as if he had done me a great favor.

In prison, inmates, guards, and the system are all trying to get something over on someone at one time or another. You have to be alert and aware of all possibilities or you can lose the little you have. Scams run the gamut from simple card games to intricately designed ploys designed to swindle you or dupe you into doing something. For example, in a card game, three guys get together and plot to raise the pot (food items, mostly). They get the victim to put in more and more, hoping he will win the big prize. Using signals, the other three allow one in their party to win by throwing in their hands after the victim has folded. Later they split the food. "Protection" is another scam which preys on the very old, weak, infirm, or young who have some money. Two or more inmates get together and find someone who meets those criteria and then one of them seriously threatens the victim, maybe even roughing him up a bit. Along comes the "hero," who rescues the victim, who is so grateful that he offers food or other items from the inmate store by way of thanks. Later, the "hero" suggests that he protect the victim from the "bully." The victim is usually happy to take him up on the offer and gets his parents, girlfriends, or friends to send money to help. (This happened to the Mafia Boss, John Gotti.) Duping kids facing years of prison time is another common scam. If a lifer has a grudge against someone, but they don't want to be charged with assault or lose the relatively comfortable living arrangements they have cultivated over the years, they hire a "torpedo"—a young, tough kid who wants to make a name for himself—into doing their dirty work, convincing them that they will gain stature that way and offering them material goods and group acceptance. These are but a few of dozens of scams and ploys used in prisons.

To me, the banana I was holding represented another scam. I knew that banana was not the one I had given Ben that morning. My choice was simple. I could drop the issue as another lesson learned or I could confront Ben. I decided to talk to him because had I been someone else, this maneuver could have ended in a physical confrontation. I felt that Ben needed to know what the consequences could have been and that I knew he had exchanged bananas.

When I told him that he gave me the wrong piece of fruit he insisted that he had given me the correct one. After several minutes we concluded that his cellmate had exchanged the bananas and had eaten mine. Ben had figured this out but, trying to avoid a conflict, had hoped that I wouldn't mind having a brown banana. At least now he knew that I knew.

That was two years ago.

IN THE INTERVENING TIME Ben slowly began to show an interest in Buddhist practice. Recently, I asked him why he decided to become a Buddhist. He gave a very reasoned response: "There were three reasons. First of all it makes sense to me and therefore it feels right. Another was your kindness and awareness that was evident when you gave me those envelopes. And of course that banana helped too. It became a lesson for me. You could have seriously confronted me with that issue. You made me see that the banana was not important, but my action was. Before, I would never have considered the cause and effect of my actions. Now I have a much better grasp of that concept. Today there are even more reasons why I am a Buddhist. Go back to a precise point where it all started and you'll find a banana somewhere in there." A big smile accompanied his philosophical perspective. That was the way Ben was.

Everyone can identify at least one event in their life where something occurred that altered the course of their lives. It's easiest to see when it's big, dramatic, and, usually, bad: a cataclysm, an accident, a death, or an act of violence. For some reason it is harder to identify those events that cause great change if they are not negatively charged. For Ben, it had do with some envelopes and a banana—but there was an even bigger example too.

SOME TIME LATER, when I was in the day room, I happened to glance up to the second tier and saw Ben walking toward the stairs. He stopped off at the communal bathroom then came down to the day room. I sensed that something was wrong and decided to intercept him. I greeted him and saw immediately that his usual smile was absent. He had a notebook under his arm and a pencil in his hand. I asked him to sit for a minute, which he did. I kept up a long line of banal chatter until we were told to lock down for the night.

I saw Ben again the following day at dinner. He still had an uncharacteristically serious expression. He was quiet and kept glancing at me in a quizzical way. I finally asked him what was going on. Thinking carefully, Ben looked up from his dinner tray and told me a chilling story:

Last night I'd had it, Calvin. Every day people try to intimidate me, threaten me, try to hurt me. The names they use, the abuse, is unrelenting. Most of the time I know that there is something that I'm doing that causes people to react to me. But I can't be responsible for how others behave. Everywhere I go, no matter what I do, I get hassled. The one person who treats me like a human being is you. My only refuge is you and the weekly Buddhist practice. Most of the time that's enough to keep my sanity. Sometimes though, being forced to acquiesce in the face of every bully who comes along is too much. Calvin, the persecution is relentless.

Yesterday at the gym I was playing volleyball and the guy in the corner cell in our unit kept goading me. When I ignored him as I usually do, his verbal abuse escalated to calling me *bitch*, *punk*, *faggot* in front of everyone. People were looking at me waiting for me to respond, but I didn't do anything. He started threatening me, telling me to look out because he was going to get me in the bathroom. Finally, I'd had it and stopped playing volleyball. I couldn't leave until "movement" [the designated time when inmates can go from one area to another in the prison] so this guy kept following me, trying to push my buttons.

What he didn't know was that I had had enough. Something snapped. I went back to my cell, arranged my stuff, packed up my personal letters. I thought about it some more—and decided to kill this guy. Everything I'd experienced since I came to prison all rushed together into one sharp, hot point.

I got a long pencil and a washcloth. I was going to stab him, then wipe off the blood with the cloth and flush them down the toilet. If I did this quickly, no one would know what had happened until it was too late. The evidence would be gone and it would be considered just another inmate conflict. I know now that my thinking was all wrong, but at the time I wasn't myself. I carried the pencil, concealed the washcloth in my notebook, and went downstairs to teach this guy a lesson.

Then you came along. Somehow you knew there was something going on because you are always aware of everything going on around you. I thought that if I waited long enough, you'd go away, but no, you kept asking stupid questions—*Did you get mail? What kind? From who? How was work? Did you work out today? Did you like dinner?* You just would not let me go. Because I respected you so much, I couldn't get up and leave. Then the guards told us all to go to bed and lock down for the night. Still, you wouldn't let me go by myself. You escorted me to my cell, still talking about nothing, smiling as if this world was the most beautiful place to be. You patted me on the shoulder and said good night.

Calvin, you saved two lives last night. His and mine, and you didn't even seem to notice. I would be in serious trouble and another person would be hurt . . . at the least. I wouldn't be getting out of prison anytime soon either. Thank you.

At the end of this speech Ben looked exhausted. His food was untouched, and he was staring at the table with an air of wonderment and discovery. He looked like he had just stepped back from a deep abyss.

I was worried about what the incident Ben had just told me about would do to his indomitable spirit. But I'm not concerned anymore. Ben is more dedicated to his practice than ever before. He still smiles a lot, but it's a wiser smile. He is much more mindful of his surroundings and seems to be happier with himself.

When I see him walk through the prison courtyard, I, too, smile. I'm glad to know he will be going home some day.

FORTY-NINE

IMAGINE, FOR A MOMENT, living in a 60-square-foot room. Put in that room a steel table, shelves and coat racks, a steel bench bolted to the floor, bunk beds running the width of the room, and a TV stand against one wall and a ladder on the opposite wall. This leaves about 28 square feet of unobstructed floor space. Now add to this two people— yourself and a cellmate.

In prison jargon, a cellmate is called a *celly*. On average, a new celly—bringing with him a whole new personality you have to adjust to—arrives once every four months. A great celly makes for an easy and relaxed time. A good celly can be interesting but also sometimes challenging considering the size of a cell and the amount of time one spends in the company of a celly. A bad celly, who either constantly steals from you, smells bad, sleeps all day and is up all night making noise, or breaks rules and brings attention from the authorities to the cell, can seriously affect the quality of the time one does in prison. The *really bad* celly is the nightmare of intimidation or violence, mental illness, or a combination of all the above. I have had forty-nine cellies of every description.

The really bad cellies make me appreciate the really good ones. The opportunity to practice loving-kindness with a celly is endless. At the same time, when you are kind, it is considered a sign of weakness and you can be taken advantage of. If you are fair and share not just the meager space but the possessions you acquire over time, you can end up losing hard-earned material items. To look past the difficulty of living in such close proximity to a total stranger, you have to come to terms with your karma. Doing so with a sense of humor ensures that you will not end up being the type of person that no one can stand.

SEVERAL YEARS AGO, a celly was moved into my cell while I was at work. He couldn't speak any English. At first I thought that this was a blessing—but this idea was squashed on our first day together. After introducing myself, we lay on our bunks waiting for dinner to be called. In the relative quiet, I heard a deep and very long sigh from my celly. I recall thinking that he must be glad to be settled in. Then he sighed again. A deep, long, dramatic sigh. Then another and another and another. Since I couldn't ask him what was going on, at first I tried to ignore it. Then I caught myself counting sighs. I tried to use the sighs as a kind of mantra, a focal point of concentration, but they seemed to chip away at my mind like a little rock hammer on the face of a cliff—and after about three days, it really started to get to me.

I concluded that his sighs reflected his sadness about being in prison and his desire to be free. I talked to some of his friends and learned that he was leaving within two weeks. Thinking I could endure anything for two weeks, I settled down to wait out his time. But the sighs became as insistent as a dripping faucet. As his release date approached, the number of sighs increased in length, frequency, and volume. I was going crazy! I finally asked him not to sigh all the time and mimicked his behavior so he would understand what I meant. He stopped for about ten minutes. The silence was exquisite. Then, tentatively, softly, a little sigh. Then two more in rapid succession. Soon he was sighing as much as before.

When he left to go home, we shook hands and I returned to my cell. Closing the door, I looked around the small space and, to my shock and horror, I inadvertently sighed. I wanted to cry. I returned from work the next day in trepidation of what new challenge would be visited upon me in the cell.

ANOTHER CELLY was already stationed up on his bunk when I first met him. This one was very social and spoke English. I introduced myself and told him what my schedule was in terms of work and activities so that he could figure out what he wanted to do and the times he could get quiet cell time away from everyone. I also offered him the use of my TV and radio and let him know that he could help himself to tea or coffee. As I did for many other cellies before him, I bought him shampoo, soap, and other hygiene items in case he wasn't able to afford them himself.

Some inmates, despite the fact that they are in prison, always seem to come out ahead, even when things look like they're falling apart. For other inmates, no matter how hard they try, everything ends in failure. This celly was such a person. His whole life was a train-wreck. He had nothing positive going for him and that was reflected in the way he spoke and the way he acted. I tried more than once to show him how his speech and actions had an effect; but to no avail. He was his own worst enemy. Just when things began to look like they were going his way, he would say or do something that would sabotage it. Then he would blame everyone but himself.

My new celly was happy to help himself to my coffee, but he also gave it away to his friends. Before long I was buying much more coffee than I was drinking. I was angry and felt hurt.

I reflected on this. It became clear to me that this cellmate was teaching me not only the obvious attachment lessons I learn from nearly every celly, but was also teaching me about motivation. I offered to help him with necessities and sort of expected him to be grateful and not abuse the situation—I gave those things with strings attached. I had expectations. If I had given those things freely, it would not have bothered me what he did with them or if he took coffee from me to give to his friends.

Instead of beating him up—which is the common prison response in such a circumstance—I simply sat down with him at a time when I thought he would listen and told him how much it bothered me that he abused my kindness, not because I lost some material things, but because I was concerned for him and the effects that his doing these things would have on him. Being angry at everyone, stealing from me, threatening those around him, all this contributed to his suffering, although he couldn't recognize this. I tried to explain that though I had much to be thankful for, a lot of that could be attributed to my making a concerted effort not to be the source of suffering. I told him that I had learned that whenever I succumbed to the powerful pull of anger, one thing after another happened that caused me more misery and problems. On the other hand, the more I learned to use skillful means to resolve conflicts and the more I used humor or kindness to cut through anger, then the more the direction of my circumstances changed and inevitably turned out better.

We discussed how easy it is to fall into the trap of old habit patterns because they have the comfort of familiarity. Changing requires admitting that a lifetime of reacting out of anger and fear is no more than misplaced and wasted effort and energy. It's like pouring more and more money into a war: The greater the investment, the harder it is to get out. Explaining all this was difficult, but it was effective. My coffee stopped disappearing.

SOMETIMES I TRIED to select someone who might be compatible as a celly. Once I was looking around for a good possibility when a prisoner approached me and asked if he could move in. Intuitively I was hesitant, but I reluctantly agreed to a cell move. It was better than the possibility of getting a New Guy with all kinds of mental or addiction problems. After my new celly settled in, I told him that he was welcome to use my TV and other appliances. I asked only that he not push on the TV buttons too hard or surf the channels as this would eventually cause the channel buttons to collapse. He said he would respect my stuff.

Nonetheless, more often than not, I caught him surfing through the channels. What was really alarming was that he would exert a tremendous amount of force as he pushed the buttons. I told him that if he pressed on his leg as often and as hard as he pushed on the TV buttons, he would have a serious bruise.

One day I came back from work and my celly met me on the stairs. Apologizing profusely, he admitted to pushing in one of the channel buttons and breaking it. Now, in the past, something like this would have caused me to explode in anger. Fortunately, my practice has taught me how to breathe deeply in order to calm the mind before speaking. I did my best to do this. I accepted with resignation the fact that stuff happens, and said that at least we could still change the channels in one direction. I asked that he be more careful and let it go at that. One week later I was met again by a very sheepish-looking celly. I knew he was going to tell me that he broke the other channel button, and he did.

I sent my TV out to be repaired (this is possibe, even in prison). But due to mix-ups and complications, it took over four months to get it sent back to me. In that time, my celly moved to another cell, one that had a TV—he said he couldn't live without one—and I missed the coverage of the Olympics. The hidden blessing was that subsequent cellies didn't want to hang out in my cell since there was no TV and that enabled me to extend my meditation sittings.

There's the potential for something positive in most every situation.

JUST A FEW CELLIES AGO an older man moved in with me. His hair was sparse and the little he had looked as if he had just passed through a wind tunnel. Years of doing hard drugs had rotted his teeth, and he wore dentures. He told me the day he moved in that he was a carnie, a person who traveled with and worked in carnivals. My heart sank when he told me that he slept under the merry-go-round because he did not have a trailer to live in while on the road with various carnivals. I was concerned. Justifiably, as it turned out.

Every night when he entered the cell, my celly pulled out his false teeth and threw them on a shelf. With the same hand he would touch the TV buttons, the doorknob, and various other parts of the cell that I also had to touch. He never washed his hands after using the toilet. As he lay in bed, his long hair fell out strand by strand and would float down onto my pillow or fall on my face. His underwear was so loose that when he would swing his legs over the side of his bunk to get down, the rest of him would just dangle freely in the open, as if this were socially acceptable behavior. When I let him know that having me view his various body parts was not my cup of tea, he would contritely say, in his deep, gravely carnie voice, "I'm sorry." Those words became his trademark.

When I got him to shower, he would come back and throw his old underwear in the corner near his laundry bag. If the underwear hit the wall first, they would often just stick there. I'd come into the cell and see a pair of dirty, stained underwear stuck to the wall and wonder how they managed to defy gravity. I would point to the clinging eyesore, and his response was the predictable, "I'm sorry." Here was a mature man, just five years younger than me, who had to be told to bathe and to remove his underwear from the wall.

Just before he moved on to another institution, he left me with one last memorable experience. As he prepared to leave, he showered, packed his stuff in a box, grabbed a toothbrush, applied a big glob of toothpaste, and began brushing his false teeth, which were in his mouth. I lay on my bunk and wondered what he planned to do with the sudsy mixture since the bathrooms were down the hall. After some vigorous brushing, he grabbed his coffee cup, which was half full of pitch-black coffee, took a big swig, swirled the coffee and toothpaste concoction in his mouth and swallowed. I recoiled in disgust and asked him what he was doing.

"It's a way to brush my teeth and get my coffee down," he said.

Though I was very glad to see him go, I have to admit that I really did learn more from him than many other cellies. Perhaps the most important thing I gained from this experience was a sense of gratitude. For whatever reason, by whatever force, I have been blessed with a life that does not include some of the difficulties that this celly faced in his life. I can keep myself and my underwear clean and off the walls. No one has to ask me to adjust my clothes in order not to embarrass myself. I have never had to sleep under a greasy amusement ride night after night. When he walked out the door to leave, I was happy to hear him say that I had been a good celly to him. For that, I'm *not* sorry.

AS I WRITE THIS, I have my forty-ninth celly. He likes to sleep in the mornings when I do most of my writing. That seems to dampen my creative process. He only has about five months left in his sentence. We are on two different paths. He is a short-timer and I have been down a long time with a few more years to go. It's the difference between a sprinter and a long-distance runner. He doesn't have to pace himself. I do. I find it extremely difficult to adjust to his sporadic schedule. He prefers staying in the unit, and I don't. He would rather sit in the cell talking or socializing. I enjoy quiet whenever I can get it.

My life has changed now that he is my celly. But then, that has been true of all forty-nine cellies. I owe each of them a bow of gratitude for constantly reminding me that it is easy to give in to frustration. It is easy to become bitter.

It is much more difficult, but endlessly more rewarding, to be humble and to transform raw emotions into loving-kindness.

BULLDOG AND CHRISTMAS

IT IS HARD to like a man who is loud and obnoxious.

Bulldog was not only loud and obnoxious, he was big and strong as well. Few people dared to mess with him and he knew it. His massive shoulders supported an unbelievably big head haloed by an electrified afro. When he walked toward you the overall effect was like being in the path of an oncoming train at night without headlights. I'd never actually seen him hurt anyone—but I knew prisoners who were afraid of him and others who avoided him like bad breath.

I made sure to stay far from him as well. Not out of fear, mind you—after all, Bulldog never gave me any reason to fear him. I just don't like to be near loud, aggressive types.

For years I had no real reason to associate with him on any level.

Christmas season came (as it does each year) and most inmates were not looking forward to the holiday period. Historically, there are more fights and conflicts in prison during this time than any other time of the year. Emotions run high as prisoners think of Christmases past, of families, and of times around the Christmas tree. In most prisons there is almost nothing special done during this challenging time. In our case there is a holiday meal: a regular old meal made "festive" by the addition of cranberry sauce and stuffing.

After the meal we pass through a line where they give us a paper sack containing an apple, perhaps a tangerine or orange, and a banana. This fruit is bought from vendors who cannot sell the fruit because it is stunted or green or overly ripe and is unacceptable to consumers. Sometimes the sack contains a plastic zip-lock bag of hard candy. Those who are inclined can go to a Christmas service at the chapel. Food items can be purchased from the inmate store. If a prisoner has money, a holiday package can be ordered through an outside vendor. These usually consist of meat and cheese. Other than that, there is little that differentiates Christmas from any other day. I believe that loneliness is the one thing that exists in abundance during the holiday season in prison. Good cheer is rare.

I HAD BEEN SHIPPED to Airway Heights Correction Center from the prison in Walla Walla, Washington, on December 19, 1995. The prison was relatively new and only a handful of men were living in the unit I had been assigned to. My personal clothes and property were still in transit and because of the pending holiday I could not expect to see any of it until sometime in January or February. My inmate account could not be activated for at least two weeks, which meant I was without funds.

All of us spent the holiday time in the nearly empty unit with nothing to do and not even a Christmas card or any other traditional trapping of Christmas to mark this as a special occasion. Since the chapel had not yet been built, there was a service offered for a maximum of 120 men due to capacity limitations. I don't know what the other 1,000 men did for the holidays, but I read a book and tried not to reflect on this, the worst Christmas of my life. I vowed then and there I would not let a Christmas pass in this way again.

The next Christmas I went to several friends and asked them to help me put on a Christmas party. By then we were all better able to contribute various types of snacks and drinks. Someone in the library where I worked discarded a thick stack of wrapping paper. I brought it back to my cell and found that half was Christmas paper. I gathered whatever I had of value, things like a jar of coffee, candy, and shampoo. These I wrapped up and numbered, later giving a number to each invited guest as they arrived. Using the donated meat and cheese from our Hickory Farms holiday package, we made platters as well as bean dips, homemade honey-mustard, and fruit punch. We invited as many men as we could and, if I may say so myself, had a wonderful time. At the end of the party everyone with a number received a correspondingly numbered, beautifully wrapped gift. Our party was the talk of the prison for a year.

THREE WEEKS before my third Christmas here, Bulldog moved into my unit on the same side as me. It was now impossible to ignore him. He had not changed; he was still loud and aggressive. We also worked at the same industry job. At best we were associates.

It was the time of year that everyone was gearing up for what was now billed as the "Traditional Christmas Party." On several occasions Bulldog mentioned that he had heard about our parties, but I never entertained the thought of inviting him. Days before the party, I invited everyone from the previous year and several more. When I passed Bulldog's cell something made me stop. I went back and, straight out, invited him to our party. His response was suspicious.

"Why you invite me?" he grunted from his doorway. Hoping to avoid a long conversation, I told him that it was a way for me to practice Buddhism.

"Oh, you're a Booty-hist!?" he laughed.

"Yes, something like that," I replied as I moved away.

When they heard what I had done, two people decided that they would not attend. Others had serious reservations. I went ahead with the plans and hoped for the best.

By this time I had invented a recipe for baking a cake using my reading lamp and the ingredients available to me through the Inmate Store. I blended three mini boxes of Rice Krispies with melted Rocky Road candy bars and pressed them into a bowl to set. Meanwhile, I melted bars of milk chocolate and added a tablespoon of strong hot coffee. Once the Rice Krispie mixture set, I turned it out of the bowl upside down and frosted it with the melted chocolate. When that hardened, I pressed the edge of a ruler into the frosting to make an indentation representing slices. On the edge of the cake and between each slice I pressed a coffee cordial. I made a large pile of chocolate shavings from a candy bar and sprinkled these all over the cake. In the center I pressed in a candied cherry extracted from a chocolate-covered cherry that the Inmate Store sold during the holidays. The overall effect was impressive and looked, if I may say so myself, as if it had been purchased at a bakery. In addition, with the help of friends, we made a variety of candy clusters and desserts.

Again we had wrapped gifts and everyone got something, including Bulldog. It was interesting that all those who attended were dressed in their best "civilian" clothes and made an extra effort to make this a special time for all. Throughout the party Bulldog was quiet and nice to everyone. He got the most animated when we called out the numbers for the gifts. When he received his he was like a child at Christmas! Later he told me that he thoroughly enjoyed himself.

Bulldog was moved to another prison after that Christmas party. Three years later I saw him again. He was being transferred to another facility and was nearing the end of his prison term. When he saw me he rushed up and gave me a huge hug and flashed an uncharacteristic smile. He shook his head and slapped me roughly on the back—nearly knocking me to the ground. Yelling loud enough for everyone in the next county to hear, he let me know how much that Christmas meant to him and that in all his years in prison *that* was his best memory. He hugged me again, which almost killed me, and took off saying as he went that he now knew what Booty-hists were.

"Oh?" I yelled. "What are we?"

"Santa Clauses without the suit!" he shouted, then laughed and walked out of my life.

REGARDLESS OF RELIGION OR SITUATION, Christmas can be a time of love, understanding, community, and compassion. Seeing Bulldog that last time, I really learned that each of us, no matter how unpleasant we may seem to be, needs a bit of Christmas now and again.

A LITTLE CLOSER
TO HOME

PRISON LIFE in America is a unique and distinctive subculture. Prison has its own rules, its own social order, and its own expectations. There are about six things prisoners discuss: Crime and Time, Sex, Drugs, Legal Work, Sports, and Food. Other subjects crop up occasionally, but by and large, conversations tend to revolve around those topics. It is rare for two prisoners to sit down and have a conversation about world affairs, music, art, books, travel, or other topics pertaining to culture. It is rarer still to talk with someone about feelings and emotions. To expose yourself in this manner is not wise in a setting where hate-mongers sit in wait for a chance to capitalize upon your vulnerability. If you have a bit more education than Sandbox 101 and if you have experiences that exceed the limits of an armchair and a remote control, you could be in serious trouble while in prison. In the intellectual wasteland of prison, it's all too easy to succumb to inertia and fall into the limited conversations and gossip.

Everyone in this environment knows longing and feels the weight of depression at times. Those who strive to excel and raise themselves from the depressive muck of normal prison life invariably understand more than the definition of the word *lonely*. A person can starve emotionally for a comforting word, a loving touch, an understanding ear. Since everything is so transitional in the world of the incarcerated, it is rare that prisoners dare to explore the realm of sincere friendship. Most would rather plod past the months and years of loneliness without making real human contact. The end result is a kind of slow, living death.

When I see this waste of human resources, when I hear people mortgaging their future to pipe dreams, when I see the lack of direction prisons perpetuate, I feel an indescribable loss and deep despair. The prison system encourages recidivism instead of education. I think most prisoners reenter society worse off than when they left. Moreover, the expectation placed on them is that they will succeed in a life for which they are ill prepared.

A small percentage of inmates, however, try to improve their lives. They make an effort to use their time wisely and become better people. They are determined to find a path away from suffering and are focused on things that matter. They do this in the face of great odds, despite many obstacles, and with little or no outside help. It is easy to recognize these people within prison walls. They are the ones who consistently, sometimes with great courage, extend kindness to others. They live compassionate lives and talk about the potential in every person. And, notably, they smile often. Many of these people are rooted in spiritual practice and meditate regularly.

CASEY WAS ONE of these people trying to improve his life. He started practicing Buddhism with the prison Sangha at the maximum-security prison in Walla Walla, Washington. By the time he was transferred to the medium security prison at Airway Heights, he had learned to meditate in the most trying of circumstances. In the maximum-security prison, where noises of slamming gates and screams never cease, Casey discovered that harsh sounds were not an obstacle to practice. He learned to use the sudden, sharp noises of prison in lieu of a gong.

While meditating, and at other times, if a loud sound grabbed his attention, Casey used the disturbance to pause and bring his attention back to the present moment. With a warm smile, he told me that he spent a lot of time being in this, and then that, present moment.

Casey is from Hawaii. Thin and short, the biggest thing about him is his brilliant smile, which radiates spontaneously and often. His smile is an intrinsic part of his personality and is seldom dimmed. I met Casey for the first time at our Buddhist practice and noticed him right away. His spiritual work with a teacher in the Theravadan tradition while at the Walla Walla prison instilled in him the value of meditation. I suspect he had a natural inclination to focus on whatever was close to his heart and whatever made sense to him. His presence noticeably enhanced our weekly sessions.

His sincerity, coupled with his winning smile, always created an atmosphere of friendly calm.

Around the time I met Casey, I was looking for a cellmate. The ideal scenario for me is to have a cellmate who practices meditation. Aside from the things one hopes a cellmate would be—clean, honest, independent—having another Buddhist to practice with is the best of all possible worlds. Usually inmates are arbitrarily thrown together with the hope it will work out. On occasion it does; more often than not conflict manifests itself in a variety of ways.

When two people are housed in a bathroom-sized space, they have to spend more time together than parents spend with their children or than married couples spend with each other. You have to learn to adjust to "that other person." There are ample opportunities to practice with situations that force you to gaze into the mirror of the soul. Yet the truth is, when we see things we don't like in others, it is often because it reflects something we don't like in ourselves. Whereas, if you are practicing deep listening, compassion, and understanding, almost anyone can be a "good" cellmate—or at least, someone in whom we can discover some good quality.

Sometimes everything works out perfectly. Events fell into place making it possible for Casey to move into my cell. In no time at all we established a camaraderie that helped make life more pleasant. We set up a practice time every evening and sat together after lockdown when there was quiet.

After a few months, our friendship and mutual respect had grown. We told our life stories to each other, better understanding the connectedness we share. Casey had suffered in many ways and, in turn, caused many others to suffer. Now his spiritual practice was making him look at his future through different eyes. He felt there was something better, something more meaningful, than the way he had lived before. He wanted to change. He wanted to live in peace with his family. He wanted to get away from his old life of irresponsibility and drugs. He wanted to go home to Hawaii.

BEFORE CASEY COULD BE TRANSFERRED to Hawaii for post-incarceration supervision there were two major hurdles to overcome. First, he could not be moved until he had paid Legal Financial Obligations, or LFO. These are fees imposed by the state to cover court costs, victim's compensation, and fines. Casey originally owed nearly $1,300. With the legislated annual 12% interest rate tacked on to that every year, the debt had risen to over $1,800. By the time Casey would be released from prison, his LFO would be well over $4,000. The interest would continue to accrue while he was on supervision locally. He would have to pay nearly $50 a month just to cover the interest. Some people will never be able to pay their fines in their lifetime. Their monthly interest will always exceed their monthly wage. Casey was fortunate that his fine was so small. Nonetheless, the state would only allow him to be transferred to Hawaii after the fine was paid in full.

I could see that Casey was caught. When he got out of prison he would have to find a job and a place to live with the $40 "gate money" given to each prisoner upon release. Once he had a job and an income, he would have to pay about $150 every month for three years.

Now came the second hurdle. The only place Casey could go where he knew anyone was his former neighborhood.

There, all the old temptations and influences remained. He would have to be extremely focused and dedicated not to get caught up in the same traps again. Statistically, 87% of people in Casey's situation return to prison. It seems as though there is a formula in place for failure. I had seen it hundreds of times. Men get out of prison with high hopes and aspirations. Months, sometimes years, later they are back, despondent and confused, usually facing more time than before.

The person I was living with, the person with whom I practiced every day, the person who was turning into a sincere friend, was looking at a future not unlike going to war. Maybe he would survive, maybe not. His chances were slim. I wanted to see him at least have a shot at a life outside prison walls. I had to do whatever I could to help him.

After practice one night, we sat on our folded blankets in contented silence. Several minutes passed as we absorbed the peaceful atmosphere and breathed in the last fragrant remnants of incense. I turned to Casey and cut into the quiet to tell him that I had thought of ways to help with his release plans. For just a second he smiled at me, then tears welled up in his eyes, saying more than words. An undertaking like this was certain to take up much of our time, and I was prepared for a long and arduous struggle. I had no idea how easy it was actually going to be.

The only person I know in Hawaii is Kobai Scott Whitney, a member of the Honolulu Diamond Sangha, a magazine editor, and a Buddhist practitioner of over twenty years. Kobai contacted me long ago when he was in the process of writing a book, *Sitting Inside: Buddhist Practice In America's Prisons*. He wanted to know about my experiences while practicing in prison. We wrote back and forth for years and I felt comfortable asking him for assistance finding Casey a teacher in Hawaii. He promised to look into it. Before long, we received word that Michael Kieran of the Honolulu Diamond Sangha had offered to be Casey's teacher. This gave Casey two positive contacts with solid backgrounds in Hawaii who could assist him with his practice and help him with his transition from prison to society.

The next big hurdle was the Legal Financial Obligations. How could this be resolved before the interest would exceed the original amount? Not for the first time I turned to a Zen Priest I had corresponded with in Switzerland, whom I will call Johan. I originally wrote to him in 1995 asking for donations of books for our prison group in the Walla Walla Penitentiary. He responded right away by donating dozens of exceptionally beautiful Buddhist texts.

Johan and I have been corresponding ever since and in that time he has graciously helped me, often without my asking. His faith and trust in me and his kindness have inspired me to try to be the best person possible. We are good friends and his letters are windows of clarity into what the future can be like after prison. On a trip to Europe, my mother visited Johan and now they correspond on occasion too. Yet, when it came down to it, I was reluctant to ask him for help with Casey's situation. I needn't have hesitated. The minute he received my letter, Johan wrote to say that Casey's fine had been paid in full!

I was overwhelmed by the compassionate response of those in the Buddhist community. Whenever I have asked, someone always responds. I could not have imagined this level of assistance from Kobai or Johan. Their involvement and their acts of loving-kindness came from the heart. To this day I find inspiration in their generosity and the way they embody the ideals of Buddhism.

IT WAS NOT LONG after this good news that Casey was moved to another institution. He continues his contact with his teacher. Kobai visited him and the prison Sangha in the Stafford Creek Correction Center while on a writing assignment and found Casey doing well. Casey has reestablished contact with his mother for the first time since he was six years old. He is planning with hope for a future.

I miss his company very much. I miss sitting with him. I miss his smile and cheerful disposition. Doing time is not as easy as it was, but I am happy to know that he is now a little closer to home.

ESSENTIAL OIL

IN MY CELL there are two narrow glassed slits five inches wide and six feet long. These are the windows that allow morning sun rays a chance to brighten the yellow-tan walls and ceiling. I am fortunate that my window faces east.

The view from these glass panes spotted with years of grime can be beautiful, especially in the mornings when layers of color accentuate the jagged skyline of the Rocky Mountains way in the distance. The hills and mountains that roll away from these sharp peaks each have their own shade of blue and purple-gray as the sun makes its first appearance. Sometimes fog fills in the valleys and nothing except the highest mountains can be seen. On other days, storms gather over the peaks and build up into high plumes of billowy clouds that mimic volcanic eruptions.

These windows do not open. No fresh air ever makes its way into the building. Air is pumped in and recycled and shared by 260 people, quickly becoming stale. The smell of food mingled with the sharp scent of sweat and rancid, stale tobacco smoke is only overpowered by bathroom odors, especially when beans are on the menu. Burning incense or using essential oils in vents or on a lamp is pretty much the sole way to mask the stink. Sometimes when you walk into the living unit from outside it smells like someone farted a rose. You get used to it though.

It is the noise that you never seem to get used to. Some people, like Casey, find a way to use the constant interruptions like a mantra, a gong, to bring attention to the present moment. And some announcements, like "count time" (which happens three times a day, every day, at the same time) can be used as a call to meditation. You start your practice 30 minutes before count time, and when they call count time you end your sitting without having to look at a clock. But for most people, the constant announcements blaring over crackling speakers screeching with feedback from 5:45 in the morning until midnight—one day, I counted over one hundred announcements in a twelve-hour period shouting for inmates to do this or that—that you just don't adjust to. And that's not the only source of noise. In the common room dozens of tables are arranged near a TV that has the latest sitcom competing with the loudspeakers strategically placed on the high ceiling. Men sit at the tables, play card games and yell above the noise in order to be heard. The mentally ill wander aimlessly from table to table begging for coffee or tobacco. The noise is deafening.

Fortunately, rather than just bars, common at most Washington State prisons, the cells at Airway Heights have doors with a window in them. Going into one's cell and closing the door against this madness is one of the few reprieves available. I take certain pride in being able to create an atmosphere of peace and safety within the confines of my cell, which I refer to as The House. Every cellmate I've had has commented on this. Often they would rather stay in The House than go anywhere else.

RON MOVED INTO THE HOUSE after my previous cellmate was transferred to another facility. Ron was a young wannabe gang-type who tried to do the right thing but had difficulty shedding the image he cultivated while on the streets. In time he relaxed and we became good friends. I shared whatever I had with him and encouraged him to work out to keep in shape and to apply for a job. Even though Ron wasn't particularly motivated, he slowly began to look at Buddhist practice. He asked me about meditation and why I got up at five in the morning to sit in front of a wooden Buddha. In a way that can only be appreciated by those incarcerated, we made The House into a Home.

It happened as I was putting away my soap and shampoo after a hot shower. I noticed that the contents of one of my bottles of essential oil were lower than I remembered. For five or ten minutes I kept going back to the bottle looking at it and trying to remember what might account for it. For a while, I was sure that I had forgotten a time when I had used it or given some away. But then I could clearly recall that the oil was there the night before.

I asked Ron if he had used my oil, which still would not explain volume missing. He assured me that he knew nothing about it. I asked him if it were possible that while he was cleaning The House and had the door open someone could have taken the oil and poured some off and returned the half-full container. Ron looked perplexed and said that he did go to the communal bathroom while the floor was drying, and it could have happened then. Not even entertaining the notion that Ron might be lying, I became angry at the thought that someone would be bold enough to come in and take the oil from my shelf. I vowed to find the culprit.

That night before lockdown, I walked from door to door sniffing like a hound-dog on a game trail. Suddenly I recognized the distinctive scent of Firdaus Oil. No one else had essential oil that smelled like mine. Here was that scent emanating from behind the closed door. I knocked and asked the occupant where he bought such a nice smelling oil. Without hesitation he told me that my cellmate sold it to him!

In prison, the most hated and despised person is the "jail-house thief." If caught, a jail-house thief can expect to be beaten at the least. When it is your own cellmate, it's even worse. Now one's sanctuary has been violated. A trust has been broken. A friendship ruined. The House ceased to be. As I walked back to my cell in preparation for the inevitable confrontation, feelings of hurt and disappointment mingled with anger. When I walked into the cell Ron immediately confessed, somehow knowing that I had found out the truth.

Without realizing it, I was at a crossroads in my practice. Not saying or doing anything, I lay on my bed. The more I contemplated the situation the more my anger seemed to shimmer like the air above hot asphalt on a midsummer day. We were locked down for the night. We had to be there together. I got up and lit a stick of incense and sat before my altar. Slowly, very slowly, my thoughts of revenge, betrayal, and hurt began to dissipate.

Twenty minutes passed. I put everything away, stood up and faced Ron who was lying still, waiting for a confrontation. Speaking softly and without tones of anger, I let him know how I felt. I told him that the level of trust we shared as well as our friendship were adversely affected by his actions. Ron apologized and explained that he was trying to get a tape recorded and used my oil as payment to get it done. He suggested that he could look for another place to live. Considering the circumstances, I did not try to dissuade him. That night is memorable mainly by its depth of sadness.

The next day, word of the "oil incident" had gotten out. Several people were waiting, expecting something to happen. Meanwhile, Ron was looking to move into another cell, saying that he wanted a better place to live. He was doing everything he could to distance himself from me and what had happened. Despite his behavior, I understood that this was actually a cry for help. It seemed to me he was acting just like a child who yells at his father, "I hate you!" when what he is really feeling is unhappy, frightened, confused, embarrassed.

Ron moved to another cell. At the same time he began to change some of his old patterns of behavior. He stopped being lazy and got involved in a daily routine of working out. He cleaned his cell every morning and seemed to be trying to do his time as well as possible. He finally got the job he was seeking and had his own income.

Ron also began attending Buddhist practice as well as occasional retreats, although he struggled with his conscience regarding his Christian upbringing. Gradually, Ron began to understand the importance of meditation and mindful practice. He realized that you do not necessarily abandon anything, including God, by practicing Buddhism. Instead, he saw that practice helped him develop an awareness that allowed him to view everything he thought, did, and said with a clearer view and with less obstruction.

DESPITE ALL that had happened between us, Ron and I remained the best of friends. I could not bear the thought of having to carry the burden of resentment, hate, and anger. By letting go of it, something unusual happened to me. I realized Ron was simply another being in need of real understanding; at the same time I discovered that Ron was in fact a teacher to me.

Ron has since moved to another institution and is getting out of prison in the near future. We are still the best of friends and work together on his release plans and life goals, which include being a father to his son. In his letters to me he calls me Teacher-Father-Friend.

That is worth all the essential oil in the world.

ANGER

AFTER TEN YEARS of Buddhist prison practice under conditions that can at best be described as difficult, I often caught myself marveling, sometimes a little smugly, at my own progress. After all, I had transformed an angry, self-indulgent, self-centered me, into a calm, understanding, compassionate human being—mostly. When certain situations arose, I now tended to approach them from a somewhat more balanced perspective. In fact, I often took great pride in having endured this prison experience by altering my own views and attitude. I can't count the number of times I sat smugly before my altar and basked in the radiance of my own spiritual accomplishments. And then . . .

FOR SEVERAL YEARS I have worked at a minimum-wage job with a private company, outside the prison grounds, that had a special arrangement with the Department of Corrections. The company gets a dedicated workforce at rock-bottom rates, and the Department of Corrections, in turn, makes deductions from our earnings to pay for the cost of our incarceration. In addition, having this type of work keeps prisoners in line and is used as a management tool.

For me, the job offered both the obvious advantage of a good wage as well as a means to utilize my skills and ward off boredom. With my wages I was able to pay off my Legal Financial Obligations, assist my mother, and even save enough to help send her on a vacation. I've also been able to help those in need, and still save steadily for my eventual release.

Each year I've learned different aspects of the job and finally worked my way into a position in the shipping department. In my position as a shipping coordinator, I have to balance the egos and personalities of peers and supervisors while managing to get millions of dollars of product shipped out correctly and on time to demanding customers. It can be a stressful job, but it's one that offers the chance to bring my spiritual practice into more daily situations. This too was another source of pride for me.

The team I work with is phenomenal, a combination of personalities that meshes well. Our supervisor gives us enough space to develop and grow and, in exchange, the department rarely experiences problems. The pressure, though, is constant. Every day the orders have to go out and every day there is some kind of small or large crisis that has to be addressed and resolved.

It was a particularly stressful day when one of my co-workers and good friends, Robert, found himself under time constraints to get a special order prepared for an early shipment. It seemed to me that Robert did not feel the urgency everyone else felt and was working at a slower pace than usual—and, when the truck came to pick up the material, after a long day had already taken its toll, Robert was still getting it ready.

Trying to expedite the process I curtly asked Robert why things were moving so slowly and told him to speed it up. That seemed to be the last straw for him, and he became angry with me. Both of us were under intense pressure, and there was no time to deal with pent-up emotions. I asked Robert if he wanted to tell the supervisor that the shipment wasn't ready and, without preamble, he let me know that if I wanted it done faster I could do it myself. Although this wasn't the first time Robert had spoken to me that way, this time, for some reason, it infuriated me.

A volcano erupted. I became enraged. I basically lost all reason. Nonetheless, for the time being, I was in sufficient control to help get the order out. But as soon as it was done, I stormed back to Robert's station and let him know that I thought his attitude was childish. He laughed in my face. In a flash I forgot everything I had struggled to learn through Buddhist practice—and I wanted to *fight*! I tried everything I could to provoke Robert into combat, but he didn't take the bait I kept throwing at him. Somehow—I don't even remember exactly how—I managed to get the self-control to put some distance between us. That was in early fall, and I stayed mad at him for several weeks.

Sometimes at work during that period, I felt occasional nudges of loneliness—and I eventually acknowledged to myself the fact that I missed the casual ease of the friendship Robert and I had. While walking in the yard where I do my best thinking, it hit me: I was clutching onto ego, doing exactly what all the Buddhist books said is exactly the source of our suffering, getting caught up in my own self-centered story. *I* had been hurt. *I* had been wronged. *I* had been betrayed by a friend. (And I had somehow failed to notice that it was I who failed to utilize a wonderful opportunity to transform anger into compassion and wisdom.) I had taken the easy route and escaped into ego-self and in return received nothing but more pain and more suffering.

Prison is full of the type of anger I gave in to. When I see it in others I don't like it. And right now I was not liking myself very much. Even as this realization developed, ego jumped in and prevented me from apologizing to Robert. *I* was afraid of rejection. *I* felt aversion at the thought of having to grovel. Again, it hit me that ego was up to its old tricks. I had to ask myself: was I smarter than an illusion? Was ego really in charge? I resolved to do something about it as soon as possible.

Without further hesitation I approached Robert and apologized for my behavior and asked his forgiveness. It was nearly Thanksgiving, and I did not want us to go into the coming year angry. Robert accepted my apology with one of his own and for a moment we felt like two foolish school-boys after a fight over something forgotten. I was so grateful. Yet I think even if Robert had not been as forgiving, I would have felt better for having tried and for having understood how fragile we are. For both of us, forgiveness removed our inner turmoil and gave us more peace of mind. It provided us with an avenue to gently move toward understanding.

In early December our Sangha held a retreat conducted by Rowan Conrad. I invited Robert to attend. When he came into the meditation hall, I was delighted. I was even more pleased when he stayed for the entire weekend. It was a marvelous retreat. All the participants returned from the experience with their own special insight. I learned more about how much I don't know and how far I have yet to travel. It's okay with me that I am not the great practitioner I thought I was. I'm just happy to know that I am still on the Path.

GETTING INVOLVED

OPPORTUNITY TO HELP sits in wait every minute. In prison, though, months can go by without anyone helping another person. In the world at large—and maybe in prison especially—when people do make the effort, it is usually for a friend, rarely for a stranger. People here are suspicious of kind deeds because seemingly thoughtful gestures often turn out to be a way to get someone indebted to you. Or, they might be a way to manipulate a person who is unschooled in the prison mentality of "the strongest survives." Helping someone can become a costly enterprise in a host of ways. Most prisoners just avoid stepping in to assist anyone in need. It's hard enough to get through a prison sentence without carrying added weight.

That was what was going through my mind when Donald—a man I had only known in passing—sat next to me at lunch one day and began talking about his daughter. Looking at him, you could never tell that Donald was carrying around a heavy load. He was frustrated and at a loss as to why his daughter's mother would not let him communicate with his child. There was nothing about his crime to justify that treatment, he felt. Donald's mother had tried to contact the child and her mother on several occasions, but nothing ever came of it. Donald was doing his best to be responsible. Each month he sent half of the $50 he earned at his prison job to Child Support Services.

As he talked about wanting to remain in his daughter's life and stay in touch with her, I saw a level of sincerity that made me want to help. At the same time, I did not feel like getting involved in another project that could become a protracted endeavor. Trying to be polite and sound interested, I asked if he had contacted an attorney or worked through legal channels. Donald told me he had, but could not afford the $500–$2,000 it would take to get an attorney to handle the case.

I asked if he had written any attorneys asking them to help pro bono. He had thought about it, but did not know how to get an attorney to assist him for free. I suggested that he pick out the names of at least twenty attorneys. He should then send each one a letter explaining the situation and asking if they would help without charge. In my experience at least one in twenty would usually respond and offer some type of assistance. Believing I had offered good advice, and hoping that was the extent of my participation, I wished him luck.

Within a week, Donald sought me out and showed me a draft of the letter he had written. When I read it, it was obvious the letter could use some work. I thought of all the things I had to do and where this would lead. I really did not want to get involved. But when I glanced at Donald and saw the look of hope in his eyes, I realized that he was no different than I was when I needed assistance. Whenever I asked my friends in the Buddhist community to help, they were there immediately, no matter how busy they were. I had to do the same. Not only did I feel obligated, I now truly *wanted* to help.

I promised Donald I would write a compelling letter if he would find at least twenty names and addresses of attorneys. The very next day Donald had the addresses for me—not twenty, but twenty-three. There was nothing to do but press on. I carefully crafted a letter explaining Donald's situation and wrote it as if it came from him. Using my typewriter, I printed twenty-five copies and gave him the stack of letters. I helped him address the envelopes and he mailed them out five at a time.

To our surprise, we did not get the single hoped-for response. Instead, three lawyers wrote to offer their services! Others wrote letters of encouragement. Donald was elated and kept thanking me. He was enormously grateful. I felt embarrassed, because I remembered how reluctant I'd been even thinking about helping him.

Donald picked the attorney that seemed to have the most positive attitude and began corresponding with him. To make sure everything was covered, I let Donald know that funds were available from a donation a Buddhist teacher had sent me a year earlier for special situations. From there, I left it to Donald. Now and then when he saw me he would let me know that things were developing slowly but surely. I was gratified that I had been able to help.

Some months later Donald told me that he was in contact with his daughter. He thanked me again and asked if it would be necessary to send the attorney any money for his efforts. I suggested that we send a bouquet of flowers accompanied by a thank you letter. We made arrangements for the flowers to be delivered along with his card. The attorney was delighted to receive the gift and wrote Donald a lovely letter. For me, that was the end of it.

Not long after that, my friend Shawn asked me to attend church with him. Toward the end of the service, the pastor asked if anyone had a testimonial. After a few men spoke, Donald rose from the middle of the crowd, turned around, and found me sitting in the back. Facing me, he told the story of how he got back in touch with his daughter and how a friend had helped him. I cannot remember when I felt so happy to have taken the time to help.

GIFTS COME in many forms. We all have the capacity to offer the best of ourselves. Sometimes it is not easy, but it is always worth it. No matter the outcome, anyone can change someone's life or help in some small way. What a wonderful practice!

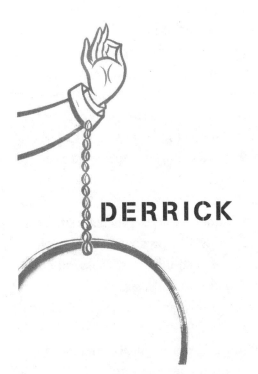

DERRICK

LONG BEFORE the speakers begin their incessant noise, before the chatter of a hundred voices start to mingle with the sounds of flushing toilets, slamming doors, and television sets, the first sound my mind grasps in the early morning hours is the long *wooo-woooo* of a train's horn.

Somewhere out there in the darkness, somewhere north and a bit to the west of my window, a train track runs east and west. Some mornings I just want to lie there and listen to the train. Someone is traveling far away. Part of me is trying to convince myself to start my meditation practice, another part of me wants to continue riding with that train. As the sound of the train engine begins to emerge, the desire to luxuriate a bit longer intensifies. The thought of facing another day in prison weighs heavy on my mind. This line of thought shifts as my mind picks up the sound of the engine getting louder out in the dark cold. For some reason, the sound is clearer when it rains. But today it has not rained in some time, depriving the scene of that added touch of melancholy. As the train sounds fade off into the west, I look out past the grime of my window, seeing nothing, and wonder how this new day will unfold.

My mind is rapidly waking up playing little mental games as usual. I get up, fold my blankets and use them to sit before my altar. Breathing in, I know I'm breathing in, breathing out, another day ahead of me. I cannot hear the train at all, only my breathing, nothing else.

The day advances predictably as most days do. Meals served at specific times, scheduled program movements announced every thirty minutes allowing prisoners to go to work, school, medical appointments, or out to the exercise yard. Today is "Chain Day." Prisoners transferred from one prison to another are bused and usually handcuffed and tethered to each other by long metal chains. Every "Chain Day" I can't help but remember my uncomfortable ride to prison over a decade ago.

THE SLATE GRAY SKY—barely visible through the grimy narrow windows of the converted transport bus—reminded me of a concrete wall. For hours we sat chained together on steel-framed wooden benches, traveling slowly east from Puget Sound into the high desert plain. The only sounds were the steady drone of the big diesel engine blending in harmony with snores of the travelers. I was on my way to the Walla

Walla State Penitentiary with about twenty other sullen men. As far as I was concerned, I was going to hell.

I caught several men around me silently praying as we bounced along worn back roads. Being devoid of any religious or spiritual influences at the time and having a great disdain for those who found such solace when in trouble, I spent the nearly four hundred miles trying, incessantly and fruitlessly, to locate a more comfortable position on the hard bench. If this was indicative of what the rest of my seventeen-to-twenty-year sentence was going to be like, I knew I had a lot to look forward to.

The guy chained up with me was an older man who looked to have gone through this experience before. He was sleeping with his mouth wide open and drool hanging against his shoulder. He had a serene look of comfort on his face, but every time he moved, our connecting chain would yank on my leg irons, causing me pain. I began hating him before we got over the Cascade Mountains.

Finally the cattle car came to a jerky stop. People were waking and stirring and everyone looked pissed off. Two by two we were unloaded like sick cattle. I blinked into the gray day as my partner and I staggered down from the vehicle and onto the dusty ground. All around us, correction officers were standing wide legged, with riot guns cocked. I looked at them with contempt and remember thinking, "Where in the hell do they think we are going to go chained up like this?" Before I could say anything, we were herded into a large intake room, stripped of chains, clothes, and dignity. Then we were assigned to a unit and a bed.

ALTHOUGH THAT WAS LONG AGO, the memory of it is still vivid, reinforced every time "Chain Day" comes around. It just so happened that I was leaving the Religious Activity Center when a group of prisoners, fresh off the chain, were walking by. Each carried a duffel bag of clothes and a large paper sack containing personal effects. Some carried an additional box. All looked worn out and bedraggled. Bringing up the rear was the smallest prisoner I've ever seen. He gamely carried his duffel bag on his thin shoulders and had a couple of paper bags balanced in his arms. Compared to the others walking by, he stood out like a chihuahua at an elephant's tea party.

The first thing I thought of when I saw this New Guy was the Grinch: pointy chin and a wide teeth encased in a smile with unmistakably mischievous eyes. Suppressing a chuckle, I heard him tell one of his traveling companions that he didn't appreciate this guy cutting in front of him. His deep voice was a surprise, considering his size. The prisoner he was talking to outweighed him by at least a hundred pounds. This little guy either had a lot of spunk or he was really stupid. Probably both. As I headed back to my unit, I remember thinking that this poor guy is going to have a real hard time.

Every week during Buddhist practice, someone new shows up. Sometimes they come in groups or in pairs. Occasionally, someone shows up to challenge us for practicing idolatry. Our sponsor, Lama Inge Sandvoss, usually handles those situations nicely by giving talks on equanimity and loving-kindness. I take guilty pleasure in watching the antagonist squirm. Just as we were about to start practice, in strolled the Grinch. He looked around, grabbed a couple of blankets and plopped down right next to me. After he was seated, he glanced at me and said, "Hi, I'm Derrick." Again I was surprised by the deep voice coming out of someone so small. Now that I knew his name I could not go on calling him the Grinch. It's funny how we get attached to our own names and labels for things. Even today, "Derrick" is not nearly as descriptive to me as, well, the Grinch.

The third week Derrick showed up at our Buddhist session, we closed the Tibetan practice by singing the Prayer to Guru Rinpoche. When we began singing, "Om Ah Hung Vajra Guru Padma Siddhi Hung," I heard a noise from Derrick and looked at him. Tears were running down his face. The prayer obviously had a profound effect on him. His response moved me to tears as well. I wanted to know more about little guy who came to our practice. Why was he so deeply moved by this prayer? What made him so open that he could cry at a ceremony like this?

Derrick was willing to tell me a bit about his life, which wasn't much different from that of so many others who come from broken homes, live hard lives, and end up in prison. Rejected by both parents before he was ten, trying to attend school while living in the streets, and at the same time attempting to help his younger twin brothers who were experiencing the same thing he was, all contributed to molding a survivor—but a survivor with *heart*. For people raised on the streets, prison is almost an inevitability. Making it in the streets usually means drugs, and that ultimately leads to crimes and arrest. Derrick was no exception.

Although he trusted me enough to openly talk about his life, Derrick was like that train I heard every morning—coming close, then moving quickly away. He kept people at a distance, especially if they got too friendly. Yet he had the quality of kindness which made me think of him as a natural Buddhist. I knew that when he got out of prison, he would not have any resources or support. I also knew that his chance of returning to prison was higher than average.

I decided to try to do what I could to help him. I contacted the Vermont Zen Center and asked if they would buy Derrick some clothes so that when released he could have something other than prison clothes and the standard-issue $40 "gate money." Another Buddhist teacher donated funds and soon Derrick received a package—the first he had ever received—with nice clothing. The Way-Home Project offered him assistance with housing and other necessities. Derrick refused the offer telling me that it was too hard for him to live up to the expectations of others.

Not long after that, Derrick got into a conflict with an inmate who had been stalking him for weeks, and was sent to the Hole. That experience nearly broke him. When he got out, he seemed to have regressed and had even carved the word SATAN on his arm. He had difficulty facing me and the best I could to do was to let him know that I still supported him and cared. With teary eyes he thanked me. Nonetheless, even after that conflict Derrick was released from prison almost immediately after that, and for a few years no one heard from him.

RECENTLY I HEARD that Derrick is back in prison. I was saddened, but not surprised. All he really needed for success on the outside was a little support and people who truly cared about him. Isn't that what we all need? He is about done with his sentence again and I can't help but wonder if

he will end up doing life in prison on the installment plan—
a little at a time. It may be a dismal outlook but it is a realistic one.

Another early dark morning and I can feel the cold that
fall brings seeping through the wall next to my shoulder. I
plan not to move until I hear the train. It comes and goes,
barely audible in the distance. "Was it ever there?" I wonder.
The train reminds me of Derrick, not for the last time. I get
up and fold my blankets and sit before my altar.

SOUP

ROUTINE BECOMES A SALVATION for prisoners who find a certain comfort in knowing what their day will be like before they even wake up in the morning. Every day the same people are playing the same games, sitting at the same tables, talking about the same things, minute by minute, hour after hour, day after day. Only a handful of people do not surrender to this easy mind-numbing existence. Most of these brave souls try to improve their education or deepen their religious practice. Some discover that they have hidden artistic talents and pursue those. Others learn new job skills and plan for their eventual release. But by far, the vast majority just sit around watching the days pass.

This environment of inactivity is fertile soil for the growth of fear, despair, and anger. Nourish this with generous amounts of ignorance, and the formation of hate groups is inevitable. Sometimes these are loose federations of casual friends who look down on those who are mentally ill, physically unattractive, or who have committed crimes more shameful than their own. These are your common run-of-the-mill hate-mongers. Then there are the religious fanatics who believe that their religion alone is the one and only acceptable religion in the world. These people go out of their way to prevent anyone they know from exploring faiths outside of their "One True Faith." The most volatile in this group of bored discontents are the racists of every color and background. The most noticeable and most vocal are the Skinheads–KKK–Aryan Nations–White Supremacist types. With shaved heads, tattoos, and blustering personas they posture around the prison preventing harmony and making prison life more miserable than it needs to be.

I was brushing my teeth one evening when two Skinheads walked into the bathroom. Ignoring me, they talked loudly about lifting weights. The smaller, younger guy asked the older one if he could borrow a package of noodle soup. Budget-cuts had more than halved the amount of food we were getting here and most relied on the purchase of commissary food items to supplement the meager meals. The older man said that he had barely enough soup to get by and could not spare any food. They talked briefly about the food they missed as they gave each other a variation of the Brotherhood handshake. The older Skinhead left while the hungry one was at the urinal. As he was washing his hands at the sink next to me, I told him I'd give him a package of soup.

He stared at me for a second with disbelief and distrust in his eyes, and asked why I was offering him food. "Because you said you were hungry," I replied, "and I understand hungry."

"But you're black and I'm . . ." I interrupted him and said that the flavor of the soup would be the same and would fill him just as well.

Looking to make sure no one was listening, he accepted my offer. I went to my cell and got two soups, some cheese, some crackers and peanut butter, and topped off the meal with a touch of Tang to drink. A real gourmet feast by prison standards. "Enjoy!" I said as I gave it to him.

A few days later he sheepishly approached me in the day room when no one was there and thanked me for the food. Then he asked me again why I was kind to someone like him.

"Why not you?" I said. "What's the difference between you and a best friend I have yet to meet?"

An hour later he came up to me again and asked, "No, really, why did you give me the food?"

"Because you were hungry," I replied. "As a Buddhist it was an easy decision for me."

He introduced himself and asked me to explain what Buddhism was. I paused at the complicated question, intuitively feeling that my answer could be important. Smiling, I told him to pretend that I had never tasted chocolate. I asked him to describe the taste to me. Brad concentrated for a minute and gave it a try. "It tastes sweet and smooth," he said. "Like whipped creamy sugar?" I countered. "No!" he said, "Rich and nutty, sort of like coffee, but different." I smiled at him like I was an idiot. Then it dawned on him that he was attempting the impossible. "That's how it is with Buddhism," I said. "You can't explain it. You can only practice it, taste it for yourself."

Brad sought me out day after day asking questions. I gave him a couple books to read. He was back two days later excited about what he'd read. On weekends we walked in the yard discussing meditation and the teachings of the Buddha. He was drawn to the writings of Thich Nhat Hanh, and I supplied the books as fast as he could read them. He took mindfulness seriously, balanced with a sense of humor.

His white supremacist friends taunted him mercilessly. They did not want to lose a member of their group and applied all kinds of pressure on Brad. They ridiculed him for hanging around a "nigger." They tried everything, but Brad surprised everyone, including me, with his response: he openly broke away from his former associates. He began to attend Buddhist practice and seemed to be transformed. He stopped scowling and began smiling. He was kind in his actions and speech and openly spoke about his anger. He began to focus on trying to make amends with his family and tried to re-establish contact with his girlfriend and their child. The change I was privy to was miraculous. I could literally see the Dharma at work.

AS IS OFTEN THE CASE, inmates are moved from prison to prison and Brad was one of those transferred to a minimum-security facility. A week after Brad left, I got a letter from someone I didn't know. It was Brad's mother, and she wrote me the most moving letter I have ever received. In it she thanked me profusely for helping her son change from a hate-monger into a peaceful and loving person. She was filled with joy and gratitude, and wanted to let me know that she and her family were indebted to me for having "accomplished the impossible."

I was embarrassed, yet pleased, by the compliments. I had to write back and let her know that I was grateful for her letter but could not take all the credit. I wrote her, "You see, along the way I've had guidance and support from many learned Buddhists who gave me their time and energy. That type of giving does not stop at one person. It goes on and on and on."

MUNNY

NINE-YEAR-OLD Munny peered through vines and thick jungle palms of Cambodia to catch his first sight of Thailand just beyond the murky river. His mother squatted next to him, his big brother a few feet away trying to calm his two tired younger siblings. They were hungry and cranky after days of hiding and moving through the hot jungle. The boy could hear unseen people around them speaking in whispers, a baby crying then suddenly stopping, everyone waiting for nightfall. Eight hours later they were in Thailand and captured by the border patrol. Munny and his family were herded with dozens of other people down a dirt road. He was not afraid because his mother told him he was safe now.

They had escaped from Cambodia! Away from the hell and the fear that seemed to cling to everything. Away from the killing fields, where his father lay dead somewhere, as did so many others. Munny walked between the soldiers into the dark jungle, madness and fear receding with each step. There was hope in the air. For the first time he could remember he felt happy.

The journey was not an easy one. There were weeks of living in poor conditions in a Thai refugee camp, papers to be checked, letters sent. The hot sun and illness took a toll and some of the people in the camp died. Miraculously Munny and his family survived long enough for an uncle to find them, get them released, and move them to a refugee camp in the Philippines. The news came unexpectedly one day—they were going to America! The land of opportunity, the land of freedom!

Munny was twelve now, and should have been at school. Instead he sat at home alone staring at the TV. He was a quiet boy who just did not belong. He hated the ridicule and humiliation of kids who made fun of him for not being American. Kids laughed at the way he looked, joked at his attempts at English, said mean things about his dark skin. He was lonely, and had no friends. It was far easier to watch TV and learn English and American customs that way. No one noticed Munny's suffering or his desire to be accepted—with the exception of a gang. They welcomed him and made him feel like he had someone to turn to, becoming his brothers, his friends, his protectors. Munny finally felt connected.

One night the gang got into a car and drove around getting high on weed and beer. The twenty-six-year-old driver was the oldest; the youngest was sixteen. Driving around, trying to collect enough money for gas and more beer, they spotted Munny walking home from a store. Glad to see his friends, Munny got in the car and was handed a beer and a joint. He smoked and drank until he was so high and happy he barely knew where he was. A babble of words swirled around him as the five young men talked and yelled with music blaring in the background.

A few minutes later, the car pulled up to a convenience store. Munny and the sixteen-year-old were told to wait in the car while the others went into the store. Within seconds, Munny heard several shots being fired. His friends came running out, jumped into the car and sped away. They had just robbed the store and when the proprietor resisted, someone had shot him. They split up the money and everyone went home. Three days later the police arrested Munny charging him with robbery, assault, and attempted murder. He had just turned thirteen.

Even for an educated adult, the justice system can be dauntingly confusing. For thirteen-year-old Munny it was horror itself. He was told by his court-appointed attorney that he was looking at twenty or more years in prison. The man who had been shot survived, but he was a pillar of his community and a distinguished war veteran. No jury would go easy on any of those involved. Scared and without support, Munny pled guilty in exchange for a lenient sentence. The other young men received sentences of eleven to thirty-eight years. Munny, because he was the youngest and because he hadn't entered the store, received a lesser sentence of five years, the first two years to be served in a juvenile facility and the rest of the sentence in an adult prison. As Munny boarded the bus to juvenile detention, it struck him with shattering clarity that he had come full circle: from the fear of harm in Cambodia, to the promise of freedom and happiness in America, to disillusionment, to acceptance, to the fear of harm in prison.

TWO YEARS LATER as I entered my living unit at the Airway Heights Correction Center in Washington State, I noticed right away that a couple of new people had arrived while we were at lunch. What made Munny stand out from the rest of the prisoners was not just the fluorescent orange jumpsuit he was wearing, but his obvious youth. Most of the men were at least 30 years old. Munny was only fifteen and looked much younger. Since there were so few of us in the newly built unit, we introduced ourselves to the newcomers. After a while Munny haltingly told me he was a Buddhist. I was happy to be able to tell him that we had a small Buddhist group and that he was welcome to attend. Munny proved to be a conscientious practitioner. While other young members would opt for gym or recreation instead of practice, Munny showed up regularly and practiced diligently.

Almost immediately, Munny got a job in the kitchen serving food and at the same time enrolled in the GED program. He awoke every morning at 3:30 to go to work, then, after work, he went to school. It was soon discovered that GED was too advanced for him—Munny could not read or write English. He had developed the neat trick of memorizing how a word looked, creating a picture in his mind of the word, and then pretending to read it whenever he saw a word he recognized. I discovered this by accident while we were reading a Buddhist text during a practice session. This revelation brought us together for long discussions about his life and aspirations.

One day Munny revealed his greatest fear: that after he

completed his prison sentence, the Immigration Naturalization Service (INS) would send him back to Cambodia. When he talked about being deported, even though he knew that he would be facing near certain death, he never spoke about being afraid for his life. His concern was for his brother and family and how much they would worry. I vowed to try to help him avoid the INS deportation order. I had no idea what this meant or what it entailed. I had no idea that I was embarking on one of the most arduous and soul-wrenchingly difficult experiences of my life.

The first order of business was to get Munny out of the kitchen. Other than learning work ethics there is little to be gained by putting oatmeal into a bowl. I worked at the prison library and talked with the librarian about Munny, trying to persuade her to hire him as a library worker. She was a socially conscious person and agreed with my suggestion that if Munny worked in an environment where books and learning was the norm, he might pick up a bit of knowledge somehow. I also felt that by not having to wake up so early Munny would get more sleep and thereby be more alert in school. Things worked out better than I could have imagined. Munny became a valued worker at the library. The librarian bought the SRA reading program and gave Munny one hour a day to practice reading with me. As the months passed he began to read simple books, later progressing to more advanced material. We practiced writing skills and devoted hours to writing and understanding the alphabet. Things became easier when my cellmate was transferred and Munny moved in with me.

But life was not, of course, all roses. There were times when Munny would get so frustrated with his reading level that he sat staring at a book with tears rolling down his face. Correction officers would write him up for smoking because of his age. Most upsetting to him was that every day when he left the dining hall he was stopped by a particular officer and searched. This went on for weeks until Munny got to the point where he didn't want to go to meals. Something had to be done.

I made a little note pad for Munny with his name typed on the cover. Below that I taped a business card from an attorney who had given it to me years before. I told Munny to carry the pad and a pencil with him at all times.

The next time he was searched by the officer, the pad and pencil were found. The officer asked about it and Munny, following my directions exactly, told him that he had been instructed to record every instance where random searches were being conducted. The officer asked about the business card. Munny told him it was an attorney's card. The officer called over a sergeant who questioned him all over again, after which Munny was told he could leave. That was the last time he was ever hassled by the officer.

Meanwhile, I was spending every spare moment in the Law Library looking into INS laws and deportation proceedings. I learned two important things. One was that a very slight chance existed whereby Munny could avoid deportation or long-term detention. This would be possible only if a judge could be convinced to hear the case and be persuaded that Munny was not actually involved in the shooting, that he was underage when it happened, and that he was poorly represented by legal counsel. The other revelation was that I was in over my head. I had done all I could do. We needed professional help.

I began writing letters to all my Buddhist contacts around the country, as well as those in Europe and Japan, asking for advice. All wrote back offering good suggestions but most did not fit our exact needs. I wrote to dozens of lawyers and law firms asking for assistance. I explained that we had no money, but each letter contained a detailed story of Munny's experiences and what his future could look like. Each week I sent out about fifteen letters. Most often there was no reply. Some attorneys wrote saying that they were too busy, but some offered suggestions or addresses that might be helpful. After months of this letter-writing campaign and many disappointments, Munny received a letter from the University Legal Assistance program at Gonzaga University School of Law in Spokane. The attorneys running the law school and some of the interns offered to take on Munny's case. At last there was hope.

A setback occurred when Munny was moved to another unit because of his smoking infractions. He still continued working, learning to read better, going to school, and he maintained his Buddhist practice. Nearly two years had passed and the Department of Corrections decided that Munny needed to be in a youth offender program that had recently opened at another prison. They had little in the way of jobs or school there but wanted to separate youths from men. Though Munny was not happy about losing his job, educational opportunities, and the friends he had cultivated, he stoically faced his future.

A year later and after six hearings, a trial date was set. By that time we had gathered letters of support for Munny from various Buddhist sources including Padma Ling, the sponsor of the Airway Heights prison Buddhist group.

Munny's family was ready to testify as well as Dr. Marquez, a psychologist who had interviewed Munny at great length. Legal Intern Scott Gambill and Attorney George Critchlow of the University Legal Assistance program were well prepared to argue the case. Finally there was Munny who had to take the stand and tell the judge why he should be released. I was waiting for the news when a letter arrived days after the trial saying that the case had been won! This is a rare thing in INS trials.

The damper was that the immigration attorney wanted to appeal the judge's decision and that process could take one to two years. Meanwhile, Munny was to remain in custody. I immediately began writing letters to everyone asking people to send letters of support to the attorneys and to the Judge.

Three months later I got a letter from Munny. The first lines are etched in my memory forever:

Calvin, I am free! They let me go home last Friday! I'm at the Video Store helping Mom. It's all because of you, Bro!!! If it wasn't for you I wouldn't be out here today. We did it, Bro!! Anything you need or anything you want me to do, just ask. You know I'll never forget you, my friend. My mother said that she wants to take me to the temple to take the bad luck out. I'm going! Cal, please call me as soon as you get this letter.

When I read those lines I was so happy that I wanted to jump for joy—not only because we succeeded in getting Munny home, but because he was able to *write* me about it. I was overwhelmed with emotion and wanted to tell someone.

But, looking around, I realized that nearly everyone who knew him and his situation was gone. So I folded up his letter and carried it around in my pocket for several days, smiling at one of the greatest accomplishments of my life.

THE RELUCTANT
ZEN MASTER

BUDDHIST PRACTICE in prison causes a person to look at himself, and everything else, from an entirely new perspective. I am not talking of the religious zealotry that stirs up passionate fervor and claims miraculous change—prevalent enough in this setting. Instead, I speak of a transformation and awareness which opens doors to understanding and compassion. Sometimes this can be a bitter experience and leads to taking a serious personal inventory of one's core beliefs. The rewards are infinite. The joys gained from this mindful practice far outweigh the uncomfortable moments of introspection.

In 1998, the Buddhist group at the Airway Heights Correction Center had a membership of close to sixty. Aside from a scheduled weekly practice, there were day-long retreats every three to four months. Each year we put on an annual event as a combined celebration of all Buddhist traditions and holidays. A few years ago, we decided to try to develop a program to assist Buddhist practitioners who are released from prison and have no outside support or financial resources. Many people return to prison largely because conditions on the outside are hopeless and the demands of society overwhelming when even their next meal is in doubt. To serve this need we created the Way-Home Project.

The plan is to set up a foundation or non-profit organization managed by an outside Sangha or Buddhist center. Any Buddhist organization working with prisoners can apply for funds from the Way-Home Project to assist a Buddhist who is getting out of prison. This assistance can be clothing vouchers, transportation, telephone access, food, and housing. The amount applied for would be up to the particular Buddhist group applying. In this way, the Way-Home Project has numerous "offices" without the overhead. Ultimately, our dream is to build a retreat center in the Northwest or New Mexico as a monastic alternative to probation, parole, or perhaps even some prison sentences. This center would house a few former prisoners and could be used by Buddhist organizations nationally and internationally for retreats and workshops. As part of their responsibilities, the residents would act as both caretakers and staff.

To draw attention to this project and to begin to raise money for it, we created a unique T-shirt design and made the shirts available for sale to the public. Because of the severe restrictions inherent in this setting, a project like this is difficult. It took years to do what would normally take months. Another good mindfulness practice—patience. The

T-shirts were well received by all who saw them, including Thich Nhat Hanh, who graciously put one on when Rowan Conrad, a student of his who volunteers at Airway Heights, presented him with one.

In the midst of all this activity we were struggling with unnecessary restrictions and bias directed toward Buddhist practitioners in the prison. We were forced to go through legal channels to get a set practice schedule, be allowed books and literature, sitting pillows and blankets, and an altar. This took a tremendous amount of time, energy, and resources. From the beginning, I acted as the group's spokesperson and chairperson. This was not difficult since there were a large number of dedicated and talented members willing to help out. The hard part was keeping the group together and working toward our goals while maintaining our practice. Not easy when people come and go.

At the end of our second annual event, we decided to use the next year's event to raise money for selected charities. Some people felt, considering all the suffering in the world, that we were spending too much money for the banquet and couldn't justify the expense. Another contingent argued that we were only allowed to have food catered from the outside for one event a year and no one would begrudge us that minor excess. We negotiated a compromise where we would try to raise a dollar toward charity for every dollar spent on the event.

Around that same time, I began to feel that my closest friend, Thao, was distancing himself from me. Two other friends in the group began to do the same thing. Eventually I detected resentment from other members. I went to Thao to ask if he would let me know what was going on. He was my best friend so I naturally looked to him for encouragement and support. He was vague and noncommittal. Days later, a member pulled me aside to express his concerns. He told me that he and others felt I was trying to use the group for political purposes and self-gain. I asked him to show me the gain and explain what was meant by politics. He was unable to discuss the problem and became angry, loudly saying that I was harming the group.

I was devastated and terribly hurt. In my mind I knew that in prison there are mammoth egos vying for position. I knew that people in prison are extremely sensitive to any slight, and that there are those who have their own agenda—which does not necessarily include anyone but themselves. For a while, I went through a bout of self-doubt. I fell into a deep depression because I felt personally attacked by friends for what seemed to be no valid reason. Worst of all, I felt the loss of my friend Thao. In this environment having a friend you can count on makes all the difference. Meanwhile, the rest of the Buddhist group wanted me to continue as their spokesperson. I plodded on, understanding better the sayings about leadership and loneliness.

Thao was a very independent, quiet, and aloof man. He did not make friends easily and was afraid to invest in any relationship. The best way for him to keep from getting hurt was to avoid people as much as possible. We had lived in the same unit for over a year before we ever spoke to each other. When we did, we hit it off instantly and became fast friends. To me, it was a great honor that he chose me as a friend. Thao was a Buddhist and began attending practice, sharing his memories of his heritage with the Sangha. We established rituals like walking in the yard and talking or cooking and sharing dinner almost every night. At those times, when no one was around, he told me about his many failed attempts to escape from Vietnam. On the night he was finally—and unexpectedly—successful, he had not said goodbye to his mother.

THIS HURT HIM DEEPLY, and he lamented it over and over. To add to this suffering, he felt that his father hated him because he took the opportunity that was given to him and squandered it. He also was certain that his father hated him because he had committed a crime and brought shame upon the family. I tried to get him to write his father, but he insisted that it was useless. From his perspective, he felt that he had been abandoned or had lost everyone he had ever loved in his life.

Seeing the world through Thao's eyes taught me things about myself I never knew. He was like my own personal Zen Master. He had a quiet patience and his Buddha-like smile was contagious. Once an inmate sat down beside us and began criticizing our involvement in Buddhist practice. I got angry, but Thao just smiled at him and asked the man what alternative he could suggest. The man quickly left, calling us stupid. Thao, my teacher, was showing me that there were, in fact, alternatives. For nearly a year my life as a prisoner seemed to go through a metamorphosis. My anger and fears were replaced by awareness and understanding. The more I learned about my friend's life and his suffering the more I understood my own.

One evening, Thao prepared a delicious rice and noodle dinner. He made so much food that I knew we would never be able to eat it all. Another inmate was hungrily hovering nearby while at the same time trying not to be intrusive.

Without thinking or asking Thao, I invited the man to eat with us. He brought his bowl, his fork, and his appetite. Without much effort he managed to eat about half the food Thao had so nicely and carefully prepared. In my blissful view I was happy to be able to feed someone who was that hungry.

But I failed to look at it from Thao's perspective. I was forcing someone on Thao even when I knew he was very uncomfortable in situations like that. I did not confer with him before inviting our guest to eat. The food was not mine to offer. And perhaps most importantly, when we ate together, that was traditionally "our time." Throughout the day people would try to corral me whenever I left the relative safety of my cell, demanding my attention with questions, requests, and the need to ward off boredom. The only time I was able to talk with Thao was during those evenings when we shared meals. I had robbed Thao of this special time that we had unofficially created. I had been insensitive and not mindful of the overall situation. I had taken our friendship for granted.

Everything seemed to be fine that evening, but the next day I noticed that Thao was not his usual self. I asked him if anything was wrong. His only response was a half-smile and a quiet, "No." Each passing day he found more ways to avoid me. I decided to give him space and stopped asking him what was going on. It took a few days, but I finally figured out that my inviting someone to our meal was at the root of the silent treatment. I approached Thao and quickly made another mistake. First, I apologized for not consulting him about the meal. Then I proceeded to try to justify my actions by saying that as Buddhists we should share what we have and not be stingy when others are in need. By saying this, I was essentially telling my friend that he was not being a good Buddhist, that he was being selfish, and that he was not sensitive to the needs of others. Thao walked away and did not speak to me for a year.

Wallowing in self-pity, I allowed pride and ego to interfere with my understanding of what was important. I let my ignorance reign supreme. For nearly six months I went about my daily existence pretending that everything was fine. The reality was that I was suffering. I missed the company of my friend. I missed the meals and the deep discussions.

During the first few months, I suffered this in silence as I went through my daily routine. Then, one day I woke up and decided that this could not go on. After all, Thao was my best friend and I did not want to give up that relationship simply because of what others said or, for that matter, because of a meal. I tried to approach Thao several different ways, but he was not open to the indirect methods I was using. I was afraid that if I came to him and directly apologized and he did not accept, that would be the end of it. It was then that I decided that if Thao was not going to be my friend anymore, he was going to be my personal Reluctant Zen Master.

The first thing I had to do was change my thinking—change the "I" to a more hard-to-define "we." I began to watch my Zen Master with what Buddhists call *metta*, or loving-kindness. To do this I had to put aside my own feelings of hurt, betrayal, and confusion. Already my new Zen Master was teaching me to have metta for my existing emotional state, to cease dwelling in my aversions, and to let go of pettiness of mind. The understanding of universal pain and suffering made it easy for me to recognize that Thao suffered as I did. His experiences were different from mine, happening at different times and places. Even so, the pain and suffering were the same for both of us as they are for everyone.

I remembered the stories Thao had shared with me about the seven attempts he made as a young child to escape from Vietnam in a flimsy boat. My Zen Master made me see not only that we all suffer, but that we all understand each other's suffering if we allow ourselves to do so. Thinking of his story made me call my mother just to say "Hi." Another lesson. Day after day I learned from Thao while seeking ways to mend our fractured relationship.

Months later, out of the blue, Thao approached me and asked if I was busy and if we could talk while walking in the yard. I was happy and apprehensive at the same time. We walked and spoke of simple things for a quarter of a mile or so. Then Thao said that he had recently gone through his classification for transfer and met all the criteria. He told me that he could be moved to another facility within two weeks or a month at most. He told me that he would not be able to forgive himself if he left and did not apologize for all that had happened in the past. I, too, apologized and we both felt an enormous sense of relief. Still acting as my Zen Master, Thao suggested that we spend time together in the present moment and not worry about his imminent departure or trivial daily concerns. From then on we became true friends.

Thao explained how rumors about me had developed and grown and flourished, ultimately causing me so many problems. I was extremely relieved to learn that rather than participating in the rumor mill, Thao had defended me. With something bordering on joy, I forgave everyone involved, and that simple act lifted the burden of hate and discontent I had been carrying. Besides, our annual Buddhist event was fast approaching and it required a lot of focus and energy.

Luck was with us, and before the event there was a sudden and unexpected vacancy in Thao's cell. I was able to move in with him, an ideal arrangement for both of us. Thao was able to attend the Buddhist celebration that turned out to be very successful. After the event, Thao and I practiced being in the present moment. I shared with him my decision to make him my Zen Master during our difficult transition.

Not long afterward, word came that Thao was to be transferred soon. Since this was a better place with more possibilities, I was glad for him and at the same time sad. I did not want to think about his impending departure. Our last few hours together were rich in understanding and meaningful companionship, filled with laughter and mindful appreciation of being able to share such a rare experience. After saying goodbye, I watched Thao walk down the sidewalk. Just before he disappeared around a corner, he turned and waved. I don't think I'll ever see him again.

I returned to my prison unit and stood there, hands in pockets, looking around trying to figure out what to do next. Several people immediately came and asked if they could move in with me. Suddenly, I felt the unaccustomed sting of tears in my eyes. I bolted for my room and locked myself inside. I looked at the half-empty cell. No Thao. Without warning I began to cry. Huge, wracking sobs shook my body. I felt such loss.

All at once, I felt the pain of not only my best friend's departure, but the effects of all the pain I had caused others by deed, word, and even thought. I felt a massive, clutching pain that accompanies the first vestiges of this type of under-standing. For the longest time I cried. Afterward, I felt thor-oughly drained, though strangely cleansed. My Reluctant Zen Master was still teaching me. My understanding of com-passion had deepened. Thanks to my young friend's under-standing and love, I am able to see a bit more clearly.

A SHORT TIME LATER, on the news, I saw an old woman sitting on a pile of broken concrete bits in a small village in Kosovo. Her village had been bombed and no house was left standing. Her face, etched and lined from years of work and her own suffering, was further streaked with tears. Winter was approaching. How would she eat? Where would she live now? Did her family survive or had the Serbs killed them along with the farm animals? I cried when I saw her. I felt her loss as my own. Thao was reaching me still, teaching, mak-ing me see. When I heard of Matthew Shepherd, I cried. The fact of his being viciously beaten, robbed, hung up on a fence post, and left to die because he was gay was not the only rea-son I cried. I wept for the two boys who lived lives that made such an act possible. Surrounding me there was a vast sea of suffering which seemed overwhelming.

The time I spent with Thao taught me much about being able to find joy in the present moment while in the midst of terrible suffering and human tragedy. I am much more sensi-tive than ever before and a lot happier as well. There is no parole board that can gauge the level of my sincerity, nor will I get out of prison any sooner for having come to this real-ization. To me it does not matter. It does not matter if I am in prison or not. To me what matters most is that I continue on this path and hope that I am no longer the source of suffering, but rather one who does his best to bring joy and understanding to others.

THAO NEVER WANTED to be my Zen Master. He was always reluctant to step forward and get actively involved unless asked. He preferred to sit quietly on the sidelines and observe. I'm just thankful that he thought enough of me to take a risk, be my friend, and teach me a few things along the way.

TYING FLIES

FROM THE BEGINNING of my prison sentence, I learned that having a source of income was important. How you are treated in prison has a lot to do with toughness, strength, size, and power. An income frees you from the vulnerability of having to ask for help from prisoners who could use your needs to get what they wanted from you. An income makes it possible to have soap, shampoo, a toothbrush, and toothpaste. Being clean bolsters your spirit just enough to feel human. It's things like that that make all the difference. Those with a bit of money in prison get by. Those with none spend most of their day trying to get what they need.

Most prison jobs pay no more than $25 a month. In Washington State prisons, you are charged a 50¢ TV fee whether or not you watch television. If you have to go to the medical clinic or see a dentist, you are automatically assessed a $3 co-payment fee. The more you earn, the more is deducted. Charges for Victims' Fund, savings, cost of incarceration, financial obligations, and other fees can reduce a $100 gift sent by a loved one to not much more than $25.

I was earning $25 a month as the Chaplain's clerk early in my prison sentence. It struck me as a fact that it would be challenging to live on the $23 left to me after deductions. But for the longest time I could not think of a way to earn more money legally. I was not artistic. My poetry was too blasé to make much money. It looked like I was stuck—until I remembered how much I liked tying fishing flies in summer camp when I was a kid. I asked about prison hobbies and happily learned that I could have an "In Cell Hobby Curio" for fly-tying. I had saved a bit over $300 and used all of it to buy fly-tying tools and supplies.

It took me months of study to learn the basic principles of this art. A premier fly-tier in prison reluctantly taught me tricks and techniques. My main area of expertise was dry flies, which float on water, as opposed to wet flies that are submerged. I liked the way they looked and there was a high demand for well-made dry flies all around the country.

After I became proficient tying dry flies, I scouted for various outlets that would advertise my flies. I sent samples to fishing shops and distributors. People weren't exactly knocking down my door to buy flies, but now and again I was getting an impressive order. My first big order was for 600 White Wolf at 75¢ for each fly. The Wolf series are my favorite flies to tie, particularly the Royal Wolf. This fly has dark-brown rooster hackle in front, calf tail for wings, peacock hurl and red floss body, and deer tail or rooster hackle for the tail. A very attractive fly. Around the time I started fly tying, I also started practicing Buddhism.

There came a time when I was tying wonderful flies for several customers including prison guards. I was so proud of them that I innocently sent samples to Sensei Sunyana Graef and Zen Priest Vanja Palmers. Both were corresponding with me on a pretty consistent basis. Time passed, but neither mentioned anything in their letters about the flies I sent them.

For months, I was puzzled. Then one day, during meditation practice, it hit me. Fishing flies *hook* fish. I was participating in the harmful action of causing suffering. The realization was devastating. Not because I was now a Realized Being, but because I had to make a choice. Stop selling flies and go back to the "Poor House" and actually be true to my Buddhist principles, or not be a Buddhist and not worry about it. I did not like either alternative, so I compromised. Instead of selling flies for fishing, I would make them for trophy wall mounts. People were paying large sums of money for salmon and certain salt-water flies. I could still benefit from the wonderfully relaxed way I felt when tying flies by making wall decorations, and I could still walk around and proudly proclaim that my Buddhist path was an honorable one.

Again, I enthusiastically sent samples to Vanja and Sunyana and told them that I now understood that the hooks were harmful and that my practice made me realize this. Instead of making flies for fishing, I was making flies to look at. Boy did I think I was wonderful! Of course, neither Vanja nor Sunyana ever said anything about the flies. I was as baffled as before.

It took another two years of practice before one day out of the blue I understood that the material I was using was from animals raised and killed specifically for the purpose of donating their body parts for fly-tiers like me. It is hard to describe how foolish I felt. It is even harder for me to explain how bad I felt. Never once did any of my Buddhist friends criticize me or judge me. They let me find my own way to realization. I am slow at times, but when I get it, I get it.

I got rid of all my fly tying equipment. Now I make *malas*, strings of Buddhist prayer beads. I try to sell as many as I can, but mostly I end up making them for other prisoners. I am not going to get rich, that's for sure. Then again, when I look at what I've learned on the Path and when I look at my Buddhist friends all over this planet, I understand that I am already wealthy beyond measure.

I wonder, though, about how many trees were killed to make those wooden beads.

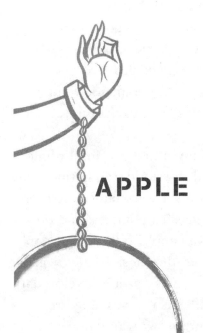

APPLE

A LIGHT DRIZZLE was falling one early summer weekend, and I did not want to allow myself to think about better places to be. The air smelled fresh and clean as I stepped out of my unit to walk the long stretch of sidewalk to the main chow hall. The wet atmosphere provoked nostalgic memories. Despite my attempt to be cheerful, feelings of melancholy settled over me like the persistent mist, dampening everything. It took all I had to face the prospect of another prison meal.

By the time I arrived indoors, my mood was sour and matched the gray weather. As I made my way to the chow hall, I tried not to let my mind anticipate the culinary surprises that were sure to be waiting. I tried not to respond to the masses of men crowded together loudly consuming what can only be described as questionable. I pushed away thoughts of those whose meal-time etiquette was reminiscent of various exhibits at a local county fair. I got into my place in the meal line directly behind a particularly hairy inmate who kept emitting grunts with each step. All at once I felt claustrophobic and wanted to run. It got intensely hot and I felt desperate to get back out in the cleansing rain. At least there I felt human, even alive.

Before I could leave, it was my turn at the food window. A tray slid out. I was astonished and stood still, staring at my tray. Right there, right next to the shriveled tan-colored corn, just above the clump of fake mashed potatoes, and on the other side of the red stuff, was an apple. Not just any apple. An *extraordinary* apple. It was the most beautiful green apple I had ever seen. It sat there like a rare jewel in dark mud. This apple had a small stem protruding from its unblemished dimple. A bright green leaf waved bravely from a perfect stem. The skin on the apple was tight and the shape was the kind of perfection captured by classic painters. It held the promise of delicious crispness.

I must have been standing there for half a minute because the man behind me roughly invited me to move on. Ignoring his remarks about my ancestry, I simply stared at this piece of fruit which seemed to be the only thing in the entire chow hall. Somehow I managed to put my tray away while holding the apple in one hand. Once outside I held the apple balanced in the flat of my left palm. Drops of rain bounced off of the green skin, enhancing its appearance even more.

As I walked away from the chow hall the rain stopped and streaks of sun reached down through dark clouds like fingers searching this way and that in the dark. I walked slowly with my apple. I could feel prisoners and guards staring. Breathing in I smelled *apple*, breathing out *the universe*. Everything there is or ever was was contained in this apple. It was a revelation! I could see it with the wild exactness of shattered glass. The answer and the question were there in the apple. I was feeling an inexplicable joy while, at the same time, I felt keenly aware. I never before felt better in my life. I realized that this moment was as good as it gets.

The apple ceased to be just an apple for me. In it I saw the long journey this fruit made to get to me. Right here, right now. An absolute miracle! I could easily see the seed from which this apple had eventually come. The growing of the tree, the care involved, the labor and, yes, even the suffering that went into creating such a beautiful apple. I was reminded of the water and minerals that went into making this perfect fruit. I felt the sun on my head, the same sun that once nourished the leaves of the apple tree. I became lost in trying to identify the thousands of people involved in creating this apple and bringing it to me. The farm workers and their families, the producers, scientists, people in packing houses, drivers of trucks, sales people, politicians, those paid well and those hardly at all, dietitians, guards, and all those other beings who somehow got involved in making this apple possible. I thought of the bees, and the worms and old leaves adding nutrients to the soil.

Back in my cell I placed the apple on my folded blanket and sat with it in meditation. I could smell its incense-like fragrance. An alluring scent. I smiled. Eventually, I was faced with a decision—to eat or not to eat the apple. If I left it on my table it would soon shrivel up and cease to be beautiful. If I ate it, the apple would be gone.

I was hungry. I ate the apple. It was delicious.

EVERY PART of every day is an open invitation for quiet reflection and mindful awareness. We can do this in our prison cell, on the bus, during coffee break at work, in front of a pile of dishes, while walking from here to there. Each fork in the road is another chance not to give in to set patterns and old habits. It is the perfect time to take the path that allows our attention to turn within and experience the freedom we all seek.

Now, when I think back to that day with the apple, I smile. It brings me joy knowing I will be walking with the apple for the rest of my life. Imagine, if I had not been incarcerated, I might never have seen the beauty that was always in the apple. It helped me become more mindful and gave me a direct experience of finding the intrinsic beauty that is within everything. That does much to ease my suffering. It is easy to see beauty in a rose or a sunset or our partner. Things that elicit feelings of warmth and joy may also be described as beautiful by the beholder. In reality, beauty can be whatever we wish it to be. When we can see the beauty in a paperclip or in shredded newspaper or an old shoe or an apple, that is when the good stuff arises. Every moment offers up opportunities to see the beauty in all things, including a meal in prison . . . but you don't have to go there to discover that.

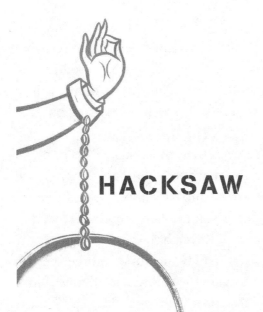

HACKSAW

IN PRISONS, the most densely populated real estate in America, it is as easy to succumb to old habits of judging as it is to slip when entering a strong current of water over slick rocks. Just navigating through the multitude of personalities is like swimming against a riptide—an exhausting experience fraught with danger. In this environment, acts of compassion are often sidelined to ensure self-preservation.

Each week dozens of new prisoners arrive, changing the face and feel of the incarcerated community. Some of the New Guys try to fit in by sticking out their chests to let everyone know they are tough. Others try to hide their fears in the anonymity of the moving masses. Some recidivists run into old friends for what appears, to an outsider, as a cheerful reunion. Actually it is confirmation of yet another failure.

This constant upheaval forces one to be alert to potential danger, scams, or the unexpected. If you take a risk and attempt to connect with another human being, that relationship is under constant scrutiny by those too bored to find something more productive to do. The fluidity of any prison population makes for short-lived associations. The only constant is the ticking of the clock.

Many people in prison see their time "inside" as a sort of surreal theme park of the macabre. Nothing about prison initially feels real. And friendships are about as enduring as an amusement park ride. Prison can be so disconcerting that it is all one can do to make it through the day. Who needs the added burden of compassionately including another person in one's life when the struggle for survival is all-absorbing? Being in prison feels like a record stuck on the Eagle's song, "Hotel California," blaring out over and over: *You can check-out any time you like, but you can never leave.*

ANOTHER LOAD of New Guys was dumped off at the prison. I watched them arrive from my window as they poured out from the staging area and down the sidewalks to their various living units. Seven guys were heading in our direction and I remember thinking, "Seven new personalities. Seven opportunities to practice patience. Seven new teachers." But it was also just another batch of guys passing through. Maybe probation violators, here for a week or just long enough to complain about how hard their few months in prison would be. Then they disappear back into society.

That same evening, when I returned from the library, I went to the communal bathroom and placed the two travel books I had checked out on a counter in order to wash my hands. Next to me was one of the New Guys. He was tall, with a large frame, and he looked to be in his early- or mid-twenties. He had a shaved head. I could see him looking at the titles of the books. Suddenly he asked me what I knew about the Czech Republic. Looking up at him, I tried not to invite too much conversation by saying that I had visited Prague.

I couldn't help but stare at the huge scar running from ear to ear over the top of his head. There were numerous other scars crisscrossing his bumpy head, and I had to ask him about it. He simply smiled and said that he always did stupid stuff on his skateboard. I suggested that he take up bowling or knitting, since it looked like he was a pretty sorry skateboarder. He laughed, and introduced himself as Joseph. Then he did something that would become a trademark, earning him the name Hacksaw. He snorted inward, then cleared his throat, then coughed loudly. He did this three times before I made my escape from the restroom. The three-stage cough program he had going on was annoying and he had used up more of my time than I cared to give.

A month later, I was sitting in the dayroom with my hobby box open sorting through a large collection of wooden beads. Joseph was circumambulating the dayroom passing by my table and occasionally sounding off with his signature snort-hack-cough. I knew he was trying to see what I was doing and prayed that he would not sit down and ask. He did. I quickly explained that I was making malas for prisoners. I then had to explain what malas were, and this led to questions about Buddhism.

Joseph struck me as a typical young guy who wanted answers in quick, short, neat sound bites. Rather than giving him a long explanation, I suggested a book that would answer many of his questions. I didn't want to get into a conversation because all too often conversations were just a way that prisoners had to stave off boredom. I wasn't in the mood to sort through thousands of different beads, answer questions, and listen to that snort-hack-cough every two or three minutes. Other Buddhists joined me at the table and as we sorted beads we talked quietly about the Dharma and the Sangha. Joseph listened and the evening passed quickly.

Joseph kept asking about Buddhism and showed enough interest for me to devote more and more time explaining and sharing Buddhist material with him. He began attending our weekly Buddhist practice and became an overnight enthusiast. He began walking around with a Buddhist book tucked under his arm. Sometimes he carried as many as three Dharma books at a time. He would read these books in the dayroom. He declared himself a Buddhist to anyone who would listen. I've witnessed dozens of captive, "Born Again" Buddhists come and go. Most move on to the next shiny thing or whatever grabs their attention for the moment. I personally suspected Joseph to be one of these, but kept my thoughts to myself.

When we worked on malas, Joseph was right there to lend a hand—*snort-hack-cough*. Often I had to re-string his work. I soon realized that he was perhaps the least mindful person I had ever met. He had the disconcerting habit of talking over his shoulder to someone he was walking away from. Doing this, he constantly walked into people. Though he always apologized, people were becoming annoyed by this and by the relentless snort-hack-cough.

People often simultaneously liked and were irritated by

Joseph. Early on, when I felt that he was not entirely sincere about his practice, he confirmed my suspicions. He used my time and the group time to help him get through the day, then stopped coming to the weekly practices. He slept much of the time and did not apply himself in school to get his GED. Whenever he was bored, Joseph would seek me out to ask Dharma questions. He knew enough about Buddhism by now to know that I could not refuse him and still profess to be a Buddhist. At the same time, he was playing cards, gambling, and falling into debt. He made bad decisions regarding cellmates, which led to serious problems later on. Nearly every suggestion I offered was ignored. Yet he kept seeking my advice.

Finally I sat down with him for a serious talk. I was direct and to the point. I said to him that no one, myself of course included, has the right to doubt another person's dedication or level of commitment to Buddhist practice. However, I felt that much of his involvement was a facade. It was just a way to be included in a group—a group that was actually doing something positive—without having to do the work or make an effort to change himself. He argued with me about that, and I pointed out several instances which he could not refute. Tears formed in his eyes and he looked deeply hurt.

For a moment I doubted my judgment. Was it Right Speech to be so frank with him? Was it compassionate to expose him in this way? But I pressed on, feeling that it was the only way to get through to him. I told him that all his life he had had it his way. When he wanted things, he got them. When he didn't want to do something—such as attend school—no one made him accountable. It was always about him, and he never took responsibility for his actions. Nearly in tears, looking like I had betrayed him, he stormed off and did not speak to me for a month.

Weeks later, tentatively, almost sheepishly, he approached me to ask about practice. I offered advice and direction as before. For months, Joseph and I went back and forth in this way. He would show great interest in Buddhism, then would go back to his card games and slack off. I would encourage him to study for his GED, then he would tell people he wasn't going to do the work just because I wanted him to.

Nonetheless, for our Annual Event, I asked Joseph to give a talk on mindfulness. True, he was undoubtedly the least mindful person in our entire group, but I felt that for that very reason it would be worthwhile for him to think about mindfulness. He did a marvelous job. Many guests and members complimented him on being so candid and astute. Looking back, I believe that was the turning point for him. Not that everything was smooth sailing after that, not by a long shot. He continued to bump into people, but maybe a little less often. He seemed to still break things just by being in the vicinity of anything breakable. His snort-hack-cough didn't stop, but he tried to be more aware of when and where he did it. He didn't apply himself at school, but at the very end he passed his final test.

Joseph's devotion to Buddhism solidified and he studied and practiced more than he had done anything else in his life. That dedication eventually made him more aware and, slowly, his problems began to diminish. He volunteered to care for the Sangha's altar and spent hours maintaining the Buddhist group's property. He meditated more often and purchased things for the Sangha with the help of his mother.

He drew beautiful artwork for our various projects, never missed practice, and became a real asset to the Sangha.

A short while ago Joseph was released from prison after doing almost two years. He is connected with a Sangha in his community and is still practicing. He left here a wiser, kinder, happier, and more mindful person. It was an emotional moment for me to walk him down the sidewalk toward staging for release.

I'M LOOKING OUT MY WINDOW and I see five New Guys walking up the sidewalk. More are pouring out of the staging area heading toward the various living units. I don't know if any of these guys will be Sangha members or future friends. But every one of them has potential if someone would just take the time to get beyond their facade to see their latent Buddha Mind.

A LETTER ARRIVED from Joseph the other day. He is doing well. It's a struggle for him, but he is happy, and he thanked me for helping him. Actually, it is I who should be thanking him.

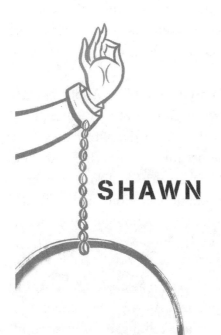

SHAWN

IT'S BECOMING INCREASINGLY CLEAR that the prison population in America is changing from the hardcore convict to a more docile group of people just trying to get by each day. This change can perhaps be attributed to the increase in meth use and consequent convictions for possession and trafficking. Addicts come into prison ravaged by the drug of their choice. Prison has actually saved many of these people from a premature death. They arrive in prison drug sick, with teeth falling out and emaciated. When they leave, they are healthier and often sport a new set of teeth.

Other new-type prisoners are young men who didn't do much with their lives. They never finished school, hardly ever worked, and lived off someone else. By the time they became adults, their appetite for fast food and material things far exceeded their capacity to obtain them. Eventually, cut off from their monetary source, they end up selling drugs or stealing in order to buy enough burgers, fries, and beer to feel momentary contentment.

Then there are those who are mentally ill. About twenty years ago, mental institutions began to quietly close their doors, and the indigent mentally ill were left without a safety net. Some mentally ill people became so desperate that they turned to criminal behavior just to survive. A large percentage of America's prison population is either mentally ill, addicted to some sort of drug, or psychologically crippled from being raised in such a way that they do not know how to function in society.

This blend of people now makes up a substantial portion of the population at some prisons. At any given time, you don't know if the person you are talking to will respond civilly, walk away, or suddenly snap, explode in anger, and do something that could endanger those who happen to be around. In this environment, the Buddhist practice of loving-kindness and compassion is challenged on a moment-by-moment basis. It takes great effort to deal with the endless onslaught of hatred, indifference, and anguish.

The mental health department in our prison often refers people to our Sangha because "meditation is proven to be helpful." We are fortunate to have gained several committed Sangha members this way. One of them was Shawn.

As a young boy, Shawn experienced horrific physical abuse and psychological torture. When he was only ten years old a family friend raped him. He was threatened by his assailant to keep quiet or his family would be killed. After several years of escalating abuse, Shawn sought protection with his grandparents. They eventually discovered what was happening to him and intervened. Shawn had to go through extensive therapy for trauma and post-traumatic stress. He was also diagnosed as paranoid schizophrenic. When he was fifteen, his beloved grandmother died. Shawn sank further into mental illness. By the time he was barely nineteen, he had become an alcoholic and had burglarized other people's property. His downward spiral continued until he ended up in the new form of mental institution—prison. For a boy raised in the wilds of Montana, with extremely limited social interactions, going to prison was no different than going to hell.

Prisoners first entering the system in Washington must go through receiving units for evaluation at the Shelton Correctional Center. Shawn arrived in December of 2000. Right from the beginning he was the perfect prison target. He appeared soft and innocent, and weighed only 135 pounds. He was youthful and handsome with auburn hair and a winning personality. All those characteristics add up to a dangerous combination for a prisoner.

Right away the older cons and prison "gladiators" went after him. Shawn was attacked often, mostly for sex, but sometimes out of pure hatred. On one occasion he was knocked unconscious and left lying in a pool of blood, beaten so severely that medical personnel thought he had suffered brain damage. Another time he was cornered by a gang intent on raping him, but he managed to escape. Shawn tried to sue the State over the abuse while in custody, but failed because he did not go through the exact proper procedures. After his evaluation Shawn was sent to a facility on McNeil Island, a former federal prison on Puget Sound.

There is no "How to Live in Prison" manual that comes with incarceration. You just have to go in blind and wing it. Sometimes you lose and sometimes you get through the day without incident. It makes for grinding days of uncertainty. This time Shawn made a concerted effort to cultivate friends so that he had some protection. He bought prisoners food and helped those who could not read. As long as he did favors or had money, he had friends. As the months slowly passed, he began to develop an awareness of who was safe to talk to and who to avoid. Shawn was learning quickly that prison life was not just about doing time, but time doing you.

Slowly Shawn acclimated to his new environment and began to socialize with other prisoners. One of the first people he connected with was Harold, who introduced him to Buddhist practice. Though life in prison was not getting worse, there was still a lingering emptiness that kept Shawn in a constant state of flux, vacillating between fear, sadness, despair, and loneliness. The prison he most desperately wanted escape from was the prison of mental illness.

After three years of precarious living, Shawn was told that he was being transferred to the Airway Heights Correction facility. Before he left, Harold told him that if he ever needed any help or if he were in serious trouble to look up an old friend of his. Harold wrote my name down on a piece of paper which Shawn packed away as he prepared to leave. After years of investing so much emotional energy into trying to survive one prison, he was now heading for another. He was reluctant to leave. At least this was a known evil. The severity of his mental illness had intensified over the past couple of years, and he saw little to look forward to at the new prison.

The prison at Airway Heights holds about 2,000 inmates. Shawn arrived in the middle of the week and was assigned to one of the three minimum-security units. He tried to locate me but remembered only my first name. His property containing my name and address was still being shipped from McNeil Island. By the time his belongings caught up with him, he was trying to establish himself in his new environment and never thought about looking me up.

Not long after he arrived in 2003, Shawn had his wisdom teeth pulled. Under medication and hurting, he returned to his living unit and got into an argument with a friend. Something snapped. All the pent-up emotions he had been holding back exploded in a blinding flash and he physically attacked his friend. In the end Shawn had two black eyes and a severely torn ear. The two combatants were taken to segregation for several days. Upon release, Shawn was sent to my unit and his friend was sent back to his old housing assignment.

No one could miss Shawn with his red hair, black eyes, cuts and bruises all over his face, and bandaged ear. At dinner while we were standing in line waiting to eat, he was right in front of me. Noticing his battle wounds, I told him that his face looked like it hurt. He gave me a rueful smile.

A week after that brief encounter Shawn mentioned that he was in the process of writing a book about his experiences in prison. I was very surprised and told him I was trying to do the same thing but with a Buddhist slant. Right away he told me about his Buddhist friend Harold at McNeil Island prison. Naturally, I told Shawn that Harold was an old friend of mine. It was at that moment that I remembered Harold writing me months earlier asking me to look out for a friend of his named Shawn. So much time had passed that I had forgotten until that moment. I pointed to Shawn and said, "You're that Shawn Harold told me about!" Shawn got a surprised look on his face and said, "You're that Calvin Harold told me about!"

Shawn let me read excerpts from his book. I was absolutely stunned at how good his writing was. As I read stories of his life both in and out of prison, I began to get a better understanding of this very unique person. He had endured so much over the years, but still had an indomitable spirit. He impressed me with his fresh and caring outlook.

Shawn seemed way too innocent to have been in prison for years. At first I thought it was the effects of the drugs, but I learned that there are people who will never fit easily into the prison role of being a bad-ass. There was nothing "hard" about Shawn. There was nothing weak about him either.

A month later, my cellmate moved and we put in the required request form to see if they would let Shawn move in with me. Because Shawn had gotten into that altercation, he really was not eligible, but we tried anyway. To my surprise, Shawn was in my cell and unpacked by the time I got back from work. We were both delighted that things had worked out the way they had. That marked the beginning of some of the best days and weeks of my prison experience.

I have been fortunate to have had a handful of cellmates who were wonderful people to live with. Many former cellmates turned out to be good friends and still are. Some write to me after all these years. But Shawn was exceptional. In all his prison years he had sought a safe and stable place to be. This was what he dreamed about. In turn, I ended up with not only a fine cellmate, but a real friend, a rarity behind bars. We shared childhood stories, and talked about politics and religion. He was interested enough in Buddhist practice to attend our weekly meetings. We cooked elaborate prison meals and enjoyed the environment of peace and the tranquility that we created.

Once more, I was learning important lessons about Right View. Many people shunned Shawn when they discovered he was a paranoid schizophrenic who struggled with depression and obsessive-compulsive tendencies. With all that, it is understandable why it can be difficult to see the person through the symptoms. Several times I got frustrated with him when he would not respond to something simple like a morning greeting. I would become annoyed when he thought that someone was looking at him and they were not. I caught myself reacting to his mental illness instead of seeing Shawn as a person with the same needs and desires as anyone else. Once this sank into my brain, I began to widen my level of tolerance and understanding. He responded immediately. The better his environment got, the better he became. This made for a more pleasant living situation, which in turn made both of us more relaxed.

Shawn surprised me in all kinds of little ways. When I came in from a long day at work, he would have my shower roll ready or would have picked up a set of sheets for me on exchange day. There were all kinds of little gestures of kindness he extended that let me know he appreciated the things I did for him. Prison life is not so different from life outside. We all want to live happily and feel safe. We all want to be cared about, and we all want to be free from constant fear. I cannot remember when I had it better in life. Sure, I did not have obvious things and could not do the many activities available to a free person, but I was content, and I know Shawn was too.

In prison, one should never become too complacent. An error in judgment can be costly. One night, after watching a movie, I turned out the lights to go to bed. As Shawn stood up, he felt faint and complained of a migraine headache. I know a little about acupressure and I massaged some pressure points on his head and around his eye sockets for a few moments, and then began to assist him up to his bed.

At that moment an officer came by and shined her flashlight in the room. She instantly jumped to the side of the door and called on her radio. The next thing I knew, another officer was there demanding I open the door. He wanted to know what was going on. I told him, and he said that we needed to turn on the light and remain on our bunks. Other officers arrived, and I began to be afraid that things were not going to turn out well. They took me out of the cell, handcuffed me, and placed me in a holding cell where I sat for about thirty minutes. Then they handcuffed Shawn and took him to the Sergeant's Office. There they interrogated him relentlessly. The officer who first looked into the cell thought she observed me assaulting Shawn. More than six officers arrived and insisted that Shawn press charges for the alleged assault. Shawn told them repeatedly that nothing had happened and that I was only trying to help him. Finally they gave up and took him to the medical clinic for an examination.

The officers then questioned me, and I told them that when the light flashed in the room I was in the process of helping Shawn up to his bunk. Shawn had said that I had massaged his head. The officers thought that the stories were inconsistent, and I too was taken to the medical clinic for an examination. It was determined there that no assault had taken place, but because such a big deal had been made and because several officers on the scene were rookies, they decided that we both would go to segregation in the Hole.

I had lived in my cell for nearly seven years. The view of the mountains and nearby lone pine tree was an old friend. No matter how things turned out I had lost that cell—that's automatic when you go to the Hole. I soon discovered that was just the beginning. I went to my hearing the very next day and was found guilty of the assault based solely on an officer's perception that there "appeared to be an assault." Because Shawn refused to lie and because he would not press charges he, too, was found, of all things, guilty of engaging in a fight with me. We each lost twenty days of good time. This meant that we would have to do twenty more days of prison time beyond our early release date. We also lost custody points, which didn't affect me very much, but since Shawn had gotten into that fight months earlier, he was reduced from minimum custody to medium. One more infraction and he would be sent to closed custody where someone like him had very little chance to survive intact.

Shawn suffered much more than I did during those five days in the Hole. He did not eat and mental health had to visit him every day. As for me, I turned the experience into a retreat. I knew that I could do nothing where I was. All the worry in the world would not change anything. Yet, when I thought about how much this was hurting Shawn, I could feel myself getting close to giving up. I had to rely on my practice to sustain me.

I used methods I had learned from teachers and my years of Buddhist training. This was a test to see if the mind of illusion was more powerful than the mind of stillness. I sat. Slowly, from the still pool of my initial relaxed state, thoughts revealed themselves. I let them emerge. They began to dance, jumping from one to another. Pictures flashed in my mind like old slide shows from some forgotten vacation. *I could lose my job and thereby lose the ability to help my mother, friends, and the Buddhist community.* Pride plopped a big stone into my still pool. *People will ridicule me and some will find pleasure in my fall.* Attachment upset the quiet even more. *My possessions will be packed up, mixed together, and even lost.* Impermanence rippled the still pool further. *Shawn and I won't have the comfortable lifestyle we've grown accustomed to.* Yet, I could do nothing about anything at that moment. Worst of all, I could do nothing to prevent Shawn from falling into despair. Fear agitated the still pool. I sat and breathed deeply. I sat and smiled. I smiled because I was helpless—and there is a certain freedom in that.

In what seemed like a minute or two, lunch was served. I had been meditating for two hours! I ate my meal mindfully, tasting each morsel, understanding the origin of everything on my plate. I did my "Apple Meditation," but this time with a cracker and soup. I ate little, but I ate well. Again I sat. This time, only a few thoughts moved in my mind. In a flash it was dinner. I ate, showered, and returned to my meditation, sitting late into the night. When I went to bed, I fell asleep instantly and slept well. Waking early the next day, I began meditating again and did this for the entire five days I was in the Hole. When they came to release me, I asked them if I could stay for just a couple more hours to finish my meditation. The officers were surprised and said that they had never heard of such a thing. Then they became angry and made sure I left on time.

I ran into Shawn at our old living unit. He was picking up his property. They had reassigned him to R-unit, which was a harder place and more secure. I had more points so I was allowed to stay in my old unit. When Shawn looked at me, I could see that his world had been turned upside down. He seemed to have lost ten pounds. He looked like a person in shock. But he managed to smile and said that he would see me at the Buddhist practice that night. It shook me to see my friend so devastated while I felt so wonderful. I felt almost guilty being so happy. Something had changed me in the Hole. I was a little more balanced and my mind felt as calm as a still pond.

At practice, we told Lama Inge Sandvoss (our sponsor for the past thirteen years from the Padma Ling in Spokane) what had happened. I took Shawn aside and assured him that none of this was his fault. His headache did not cause all this trouble for us. I assured him that no matter what, I would not abandon him. I tried to explain that what happened to us was our karma, what we had to work with. But it was what we did with it that would determine future conditions. We had to make the best of it and not give in to hate or blame. The officer who made the initial charge needed our compassion and understanding as much as we did.

Back in the practice session, Lama Inge, knowing that Shawn had not eaten in days, decided we would use the crackers and juice in our cabinet and make a food offering and *tsog* ceremony. This way we were able to fill Shawn up with some food. The Sangha came together in support of him. I think that is when Shawn began to think seriously about being a Buddhist.

Despite his history of abuse and the many negative experiences he endured while in prison, Shawn is among the kindest, most compassionate people I have ever met. I feel shame when I recall how I used to avoid people like him who were different or disturbing. I had tried to stay clear of those who had mental problems and those who had long histories of drug abuse. They just carried too much baggage. After getting to know Shawn I realized that I had missed out on other opportunities and that I could not reserve kindness and compassion for only certain kinds of people.

When we take the time to know the people around us, it becomes easier to extend compassion and loving-kindness to them. Those who are in prison and seem to be different are simply people who need the same kindness everyone else is seeking. No matter what they did, who they are, what they look like, or how they act, like all of us, they want to be happy.

ARTICHOKE HEART

IT'S SURPRISING what people describe as the first thing they want to do when they are released from prison. For many, it's a cigarette before anything else. Several admit to wanting drugs. Others are solely focused on sex, or drinking a beer. Many just want to see their families. But, by far, the *second* thing nearly everyone mentions is food. After years of prison cuisine, I, too, occasionally succumb to fantasies of fresh fruit, a good pizza, or my favorite dish: a cheese and mushroom omelet with a slice of tomato, homemade hash browns fried in butter, and hot biscuits on the side. To keep my sanity, I avoid the food channel on television as much as I avoid reruns of "The Dukes of Hazard."

My greatest concerns about being incarcerated actually have little to do with food. Considering the poor quality of medical care in most facilities and the abundant stories of mismanaged prescriptions, misdiagnosed conditions, and mistreatment by health-care providers, I fear being ill, getting hurt, or dying "inside." Over the years I've attended memorial services for dozens of men who died in prison.

For well over a decade I was fortunate to have good health, and very few injuries. Any medical concerns I did have were minor. This came to an abrupt halt one day.

On our tier about forty men share a communal bathroom. When you enter, there are three showers to the right with courtesy doors which have a large gap between the floor and the bottom of the door. Because the shower nozzles face the doors and spray water on them, the water always leaks out from the bottom of the doors. Straight ahead are four sinks with two soap dispensers that leak liquid soap. Two toilets and two urinals are to the left. The floor is made of small, tan-colored ceramic tiles. If you're not careful, it is easy to slip on the tiles—especially when water from the showers covers the floor and soap from the dispensers adds to the slick surface. You cannot see the water until you are directly on top of it, and if you are walking normally and not paying attention, a fall is just about inevitable.

One day a couple of years ago, I walked into the bathroom and stepped onto the slippery, wet, soapy mixture. My foot shot up into the air and I began to fall backward. Immediately, I grabbed the edge of the sink to regain my balance. Unfortunately, the sink was covered with soap, which caused my hand to slip into the basin. At the same time I was still falling backward. My wrist got caught under the faucet, and before I could extract it, I heard a ripping sound.

An instant later, I felt a white-hot sharp pain shoot through my right arm.

As I stood up, holding my arm to my side, a very strange thing happened. The pain began a step-by-step ascent to more acute heights, and simultaneously, I began to feel detached from my body. At first I thought this was due to shock, and I was grateful for it. Then I realized that I was actually thinking about other people and not my pain.

I imagined myself in the place of human beings who had suffered greater injuries than I. I thought of Nelson Mandela and his long years of pain and suffering. I touched the tremendous sorrow that the Dalai Lama and the Tibetan people have endured for half a century. I could feel the anguish of those suffering in refugee camps in Central Africa. I saw the uncounted thousands in Iraq, on all sides of the conflict, who experienced terrible injuries or death. A faint recollection surfaced of my father's calm when he slammed his fingers in our car door decades ago. This thought fleetingly intersected with memories of the men who suffered and died of cancer at this prison.

My pain became a pinprick of light just beyond me, less significant than before. I could still feel it in some distracting way, but it was not all-consuming. It was diminished, somehow, by the awareness of my common bond with the suffering of countless beings throughout time and space.

I inhaled, breathing in deeply, then exhaled. Not wanting the pain to consume me as it orbited within reach, I began meditating. I did more meditation and focused more intently on my breath during the next few weeks than at any other time in my life. The result was both interesting and calming.

It seemed that the pain was forcing me to discard frivolous thoughts. My mind became sharp and clear, like finely cut crystal. I began to equate the pain to . . . an artichoke.

An artichoke, like the thistle it is related to, is not very appealing. Once it is properly cooked, however, it offers up a tasty reward in the fleshy bases of the leaves and the heart buried deep within. As I approached the heart of my pain, I felt a sort of kinship with my mental projection of an artichoke.

Nonetheless, even as I was practicing with the pain, I still had to deal with the fact of my injury. Hoping against hope that this was just a minor injury, I waited a day before I admitted that there was something seriously wrong with my arm. By this time it was covered with interesting swirling shades of yellow, blue, black, and red. I told the officers what happened and said that I was hurting, but that the pain was manageable. Since it was not deemed an emergency, I was told to put in a request to the dreaded medical clinic. This is done on what is commonly referred to as a "kite," which is a note with your name, institution number, and cell location, and a brief description of the complaint or request.

A week passed without any response from the medical clinic. I showed the unit sergeant my arm, which by now was not only colorful, but swollen, and I was seen by the clinic the next day.

My examination consisted of sitting and waiting for an hour. Then I was seen by a nurse who told me to wait in a hall. I sat there for half an hour until an x-ray technician looked at the injury and said that it probably wasn't broken and most likely was sprained. I waited another hour-and-a-half in the hallway before a team of four—a doctor, two nurses, and a physician's assistant—examined me. After a few minutes, they said it looked as if I had detached biceps, and I would need an MRI to confirm it. They told me to make myself available for transport to a local medical center outside the facility. I had to grin at that—it wasn't like I had anywhere else to be!

For two weeks I waited to be called, but nothing happened. Finally, concerned that my arm wasn't getting sufficient blood flow, I threatened legal action in order to get the medical attention I needed. Nearly a month after the injury, I was finally seen by an orthopedic surgeon. Right away he diagnosed the injury as a distal biceps tendon rupture and a complete rupture of the radial tuberosity. In other words, I really hurt my arm. He ordered an immediate MRI.

To help endure the pain of lying still in various positions during the MRI, I did breathing exercises. I again visualized an artichoke. When I completed inhaling and exhaling deeply, I mentally peeled away another leaf on the artichoke. The one time I got distracted and stopped doing this, a tidal wave of pain came crashing back. With tears sliding down the sides of my face, and beads of sweat popping up on my forehead, I persuaded my mind to swiftly return to the half-consumed artichoke, leaf by leaf, to the heart, breath by breath for the heart-mind. The pain subsided, disappearing into whatever place pain goes when it's not clamoring for attention.

The very next day I was on the operating table for a couple of hours having holes drilled into the bone of my upper arm in order to sew my biceps back on and in the right location. The tendons in my lower arm were repaired at the same time.

I cannot begin to describe the way my arm hurt after the pain medication ran out. I could not sleep for days, and relied on meditation to calm my mind. Sometimes at night I would lie on my bunk and visualize that artichoke, peeling away at it until I got to the heart. My arm would feel very hot, but would not hurt for up to an hour at a time. Then I'd have to start meditating again and conjure up my mental artichoke.

I asked to return to the medical clinic, and was told someone would see me about the pain. It never happened. It took nearly three months for my arm to heal enough to use it. If I hadn't had my practice, I really don't know how I could have endured those months of discomfort. Years of practice made it possible for me to concentrate on something as simple as an artichoke, and this helped immeasurably in my ability to manage the intensity of the pain.

WHEN I AM RELEASED from prison, I know just what I want to do. First I will hug my mother and my friends. Then, I hope we will all go out to dinner. If I'm lucky, the menu will offer something with artichoke hearts.

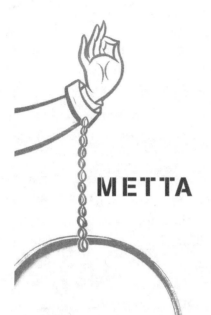

METTA

SEVERAL YEARS AGO I arranged to meet a friend in the Religious Activity Center library. He was getting out of prison soon and had no resources. I had compiled a list of what he could do and places he could go and had arranged for assistance to be available once he got out. As we were sitting down to talk, an inmate came up to me and started yelling, calling me every name in the book. He began pacing back and forth in front of me in a threatening manner. As he shouted profanities, his spittle dotted my face.

Everyone in the room was shocked. There was no officer nearby. The situation was getting worse, and he appeared to be on the verge of exploding. I tried to maintain a sense of calmness and stillness and asked him quietly if we could sit down. It did nothing to defuse his anger and the tension escalated.

What was strangest about this was not the unprovoked attack but my reaction. I'm not a small guy, and I can handle myself if necessary. Most people here know that. But instead of responding as the circumstance seemed to dictate, I casually placed my left hand on one of the bookshelves and listened silently to his tirade.

As I stood there, I felt my adrenaline surging as anger slowly, uncontrollably began to rise. Struggling to keep calm and look relaxed, I reached into the bookshelf and randomly pulled out a book. When the enraged man turned away for a moment, I chanced a glance at the book. I was absolutely shocked to see that it was from the Buddhist shelf—which I didn't even know I was near. Our two shelves of Buddhist books had always been on the other side of the room—and I was even more surprised to see that it was entitled *Mindfulness: The Path to the Deathless*, by Ajahn Sumedho. Trying to look calm as the man got closer to the edge of physical assault, I nonchalantly flipped open the book and saw the chapter heading: *Kindness (Metta)*.

Even as the guy continued to rage at me, I became absorbed in reading:

Metta means you love your enemy, we don't have to like them, but we can love them. We can refrain from unpleasant thoughts and vindictiveness, from any desire to hurt them or annihilate them . . .

I tried to actualize some of this right here—right in the midst of the cursing and yelling. I was no longer angry or fearful. My apparent calm started to become real. I smiled at the man who was still yelling and walked over to the person I came there to meet.

And, as rapidly as the event started, it stopped. The man turned and left. I felt sorrow for him and his burden of fear. I sat down and talked to my friend about his concerns while everyone else just stared. I don't know what really happened, especially to me, but I'm grateful for that lesson. Sometimes prison is kinda cool!

FREEDOM

THE SOUND OF MY GONG drifts along the quiet prison halls. It is still dark with only a hint of dawn. The sound slowly fades as I relax on folded blankets. My stomach growls and thoughts of food arise. I bring my focus to my breath and smile at my altar. My butt itches a little and I squirm. I breathe some more. A guard walks by and stares at me for a minute or so. I wonder what he is thinking. I become frustrated. As one thought ends and another begins, I catch a glimpse of understanding, too brief to fully see. My mind moves on. Eventually, my mind calms down. I notice the clock. Nearly thirty minutes have passed. I say a prayer and bow. The sound of my gong again drifts along the prison hallways.

I arise from meditation and look out my window. There is a large pine tree visible from that window. Years ago, when I first peered out from the narrow glass slit, the only tree I could clearly see was that lone pine—really, I could only see the top part of it. A wall of earthwork designed to hide the prison from public view provided just a partial glimpse of what was obviously a very large tree.

I connected with this tree right away. It had been wounded by a lighting strike, which cleanly shaved off the top, making the tree appear as if it were trimmed by a mad gardener. The tree has offered up a tremendous amount of teachings. A kind of constant in my life, it has paradoxically taught me about the impermanence of life and about the foolishness of attachment.

As the years pass by, the high earthwork wall erodes and the tree grows, exposing more and more parts of itself. Eventually the top of the tree grew out; maybe no one knows what it used to look like but me. Every morning I look at the sunrise and the tree. Sometimes there is little in the way of a sunrise but the tree stands there . . . being a tree.

I've anchored my practice to that tree on days when it was difficult to sit. The pair of hawks that reside in it made me realize that the tree was not mine alone to enjoy but something to be shared and cared about by all beings. As the man-made wall erodes, more trees reveal themselves, joining the tree in its sentinel work.

I know that the tree is not alone out there in that rocky, dry field. I have a sense of community and freedom.

A CLOSE
ENCOUNTER

MANY YEARS AGO, I was on a visit to Neuschwanstein, the castle built by King Ludwig II in Germany. I happened to be walking with my aunt through the nearby Bavarian town of Schwangau. A light drizzle lent a Wagnerian tone to the beautiful alpine setting.

In a rural community it is normal for cows to be herded through the town to and from the grazing fields twice a day. At a certain crossroads, all auto and pedestrian traffic is halted to allow the cows to pass. I was standing there with my aunt and several other people watching the cows crossing when one cow stopped in the narrow alley and refused to cross the main street. No matter what the herding boy did, nothing could budge the cow. The other animals swiftly crossed the street with bells ringing. But the lone dissenter would not follow. Meanwhile the traffic in both directions was piling up as a crowd of people watched the scene, waiting for the cow to move.

Suddenly, this soft-faced creature snapped its head to the side and looked directly at me. It stood there staring me in the eye! I felt conspicuous in my sea-blue Pendleton shirt as everyone began searching for the source of the cow's interest. An instant later, the cow began walking, then running toward me. I swear it acted as if we were long lost friends with a big smile and limpid eyes and all. As it neared, I began to worry that if it did not slow down, I would be trampled. Nevertheless, I stayed put and tried not to freak out in the face of a seemingly happy cow running to greet me.

The cow put on the brakes just feet in front of me and slid to a halt with its nose less than an inch from my chest. I was relieved that I had survived a bizarre vacation adventure, when the cow, still looking me in the eye, stuck out a long gray tongue and licked me from my belt to the top button of my shirt, leaving a wide snail-like trail.

To this day I firmly believe that it winked at me before disappearing down the other side of the alley.

I was momentarily stunned, but the crowd loved it. Everyone was laughing uproariously and applauding, including my dear old aunt. As things returned to normal, people passed me smiling and patting me on the shoulder saying that this incident added to their vacation experience.

Now, upon reflection and looking at this from my Buddhist perspective, I wonder if the cow was the reincarnation of a friend of mine from whom I borrowed a shirt I never returned.

Well, who knows?

LETTING GO

NOT LONG AGO, despite many years of practice, I unexpectedly became embroiled in a wave of hatred and anger. A
group of people had, it seemed, gone out of their way to
make my life more difficult, and I began to entertain ideas of
what I could do to them for retaliation. The more I played
this out in my mind, the angrier I became, until I realized that
I was consumed by this mental process and spiraling deeper
into negativity. It was late, and there was no chance to take
a walk, run, lift weights, or even talk to friends. I was
enclosed in my cell alone.

I folded my blankets and sat before my altar focusing on
my breathing. The act of doing this, of moving away from
the angry stories we tell ourselves in our mind, and just

returning over and over to the practice of breathing can be called *letting go*. It is an extraordinarily powerful practice.

Letting go is difficult because our natural response is to cling to things. We become so emotionally invested in them that even the thought of letting go is disturbing. Letting go is sort of like cleaning out the garage. There is stuff there that you think you want to keep, but once you get rid of it you forget you ever had it in the first place. Not only that, you feel a sense of relief and satisfaction at the results. Even during meditation, people bring concepts to the cushion about what should or should not be happening. It rarely, if ever, turns out the way we expect, and attachment to our ideas just causes dissatisfaction.

Learning to flow with whatever presents itself, without rigidly holding on to a set viewpoint or idea, enables us to be open to others in an altogether different way.

I experienced this one day when an inmate approached me and said that he did not "agree with Buddhism." I asked him if he disagreed with limitless compassion for all beings, or having deep understanding, or loving-kindness. He said he did not disagree with those things, but "people who didn't worship God were harmful to the spirit and maybe even dangerous." I asked him if he would like to pray for me. His face lit up with a smile and he said he would love to. We bowed our heads. He prayed aloud and then we prayed silently for a minute. Afterward he beamed at me, shook my hand, and walked away. In this case it was far better to pray together than to discuss our different perspectives. I let go of my need to defend my practice, and in the process he also let go of his need to prove his point.

Letting go helps us understand that misery comes in many forms, much of it self-manufactured. I have a friend who is a genius at this. At least twice a week in the communal bathroom, he asks my opinion about his appearance. He's seldom happy with the way he looks. Either his goatee is crooked or his hair too short or too long. While I was brushing my teeth one morning, my friend came up, looked into the mirror next to me, and exclaimed how much he hated the way his hair curled a certain way. Exasperated, I asked if he would be happy if his hair was perfect but he had only one arm. He looked at me as if I were stupid and said no of course not. I looked into the mirror and smiled, saying to his reflection that there were a lot of people without limbs who would love to have his hair problems. My friend punched me on the shoulder and laughingly said that I made him think all the time. The next day he asked me if I thought he had too many freckles.

A Buddhist in prison can develop a solid practice only by changing his or her thinking and perspective. One way to do this is to let go of personal feelings of hurt, betrayal, confusion, and fear and view each person as a potential teacher. The guards, the hate-mongers, the racists, people you like, people you don't like, people who don't like you—all have something to offer, all have the ability to teach valuable lessons which can enhance your practice. I have seen that with their help, a prisoner can learn to cease dwelling in aversion, hatred, anger, and other harmful emotional habit patterns. He can gain deep insight and learn to have loving-kindness for others and for himself. He can learn to let go.

HAPPY HOLIDAYS

THANKSGIVING MORNING, 1996, marked the end of a long winter ice storm. Snow sat on the ground inches deep. The air was crisp and made one realize that there *is* hair in the nose. It was the kind of day where each breath brought on a feeling of melancholy and a good strong hit of nostalgia. Memories of Thanksgivings past and carefree fall days flooded the senses. You know, the kind of day that brings you toward the brink of depression, but at the same time makes you feel glad to be alive.

A couple of hours after breakfast, I decided that a brisk walk around the institutional grounds would add spice to the noontime Thanksgiving meal. I bundled up in all of my winter clothes and set out crunching across the crust of frozen snow. Occasionally, I'd run into another brave soul outside doing the nostalgic shuffle. I'd break into his private thoughts with a cheerful "Good morning!" Most of the time there was no response, though I did receive two grunts and a snort. After completing a couple of miles I found myself near the recreation building and for no particular reason entered. The entryway to the Rec Building has an officer station located against the far wall; it's what you see first when you come in.

On that Thanksgiving day the officer in charge of the booth was a woman in her late forties or early fifties. She looked up from her paperwork, glared at me, and said, "You're from M-unit. This is not your rec time."

For a second I could feel the depression of the day begin to emerge. Then, suddenly, I saw her as more than just a faceless prison guard—she might be someone's wife, a mother perhaps, even a grandmother, away from family, alone and human like me. I broke into a wide smile and said, "Sorry to bother you, but I've been paid a Jolly Rancher to deliver a singing telegram." Before she could reply, I sang, "Happy Holidays . . ." and stopped. With a befuddled look, I scratched my head and said, "That's all I know, but I'll be back next year to sing you the next verse."

She blinked twice and burst out laughing. Without another word I turned around and walked out into the harsh, cold sunlight, softened by peals of laughter behind me.

MIRACLES

EVER HAD one of Those Days? Everything you touch breaks, falls over, or doesn't work. Everything you say sounds wrong or is misunderstood. The kind of day where even friends avoid you for no apparent reason and it seems that the next logical step in this progression is a decline into depression. What I've discovered is that when I see through all the drama in my life and can find a little space to just laugh at my moods and negativity, it's kind of like opening myself up to a miracle.

One day, I was walking outdoors when it was snowing lightly and the sidewalks were slick with packed snow and ice. Halfway to the prison dining hall my left foot suddenly slipped straight up in the air. Trying to balance the shift in weight, my right foot overcompensated and stomped down like an anchor. Naturally that did not work out too well because it went in a northerly direction, opposite from where my left foot was heading. I landed flat on my back with all the air knocked out of me in one big puff. The serious persona I had so carefully cultivated over the years did not stand a chance plopped down on my back in the snow. I laughed so hard at this absurd view of myself that it hurt. Everyone who saw me began to clap and laugh too. As I arose from the snow, I clearly realized—in more ways than one!—the importance of balance in my life.

A few days later, a new prisoner I'd hardly spoken to was walking into our living unit when he looked over at me enjoying some fresh evening air before turning in for the night. He beamed a radiant smile as he entered the building, and said, "Good night, grandpa. Hope you don't get too cold out here," and disappeared inside laughing.

I was stunned by the remark. My first reaction was an indignant growl at being referred to as "grandpa." Then I realized that compared to him, I was, indeed, old enough to be a grandpa! More importantly, I'd cultivated an atmosphere where those near me could be themselves without fear. That thought made me truly happy as I inhaled the cool night air and then took my old bones to bed.

Smiling, I enjoyed the miracle of contentment.

Sometimes, I think people look for miracles in all the wrong places.

LIBERATING OUR GARDENS

AIRWAY HEIGHTS CORRECTION CENTER is a gray, colorless, smelly place, with a wall of dirt surrounding it and speakers letting you know for hours on end that you are in prison. In prisons, soft lines and vibrant colors are limited mostly to shades of gray and tan. But in my prison, there is one exception. Someone has allowed small patches of flowers to grow in front of the housing units and next to several of the activity buildings. These are cared for by inmate ground crews who are paid 35¢ an hour. Some workers honestly enjoy tending the gardens; others only care about collecting their monthly gratuity.

Whenever I pass by these islands of blazing color, my eyes are drawn to the refreshing beauty of the flowers. I cannot help smiling as I catch a whiff of the fragrance they offer in the heat of the day. I feel guilty, sometimes, for being happy when I absorb the sight and smells of those flowers. It's like pocketing a dollar bill found in an empty street. You know it belonged to someone who lost it, yet you marvel at your fortune.

There is one rather long stretch of ground, eight feet wide and thirty-five feet long, next to the gym and program buildings. A decade ago someone made a serious attempt to fill that space with flowers, but since then, not even a minimal amount of care was given to the forlorn plot of land. Weeds were choking out any flower brave enough to show its petals. That stretch of land was a perfect example of the atmosphere prevalent in our prison.

At the end of a weekly meditation practice, just as spring was folding into summer, my friend Shawn suggested that we volunteer to weed the neglected patch of dandelions and thistles. I was immediately opposed to the idea. Several hours every morning would cut into my writing time, my yard time, and further burden my busy schedule.

It happens that Shawn is an exceptionally persistent person, and he kept pointing out the benefits of gardening. No matter how many negative excuses I put forth, he refused to entertain them. In the end, he would not let me weasel out of it. Thinking this would take about one or two weeks, I capitulated. Somehow he convinced the officers and staff to allow us to weed that area and soon there we were, tools in hand, staring at a robustly healthy weed garden.

Starting at the north end of the plot and working south we took advantage of the shade the building provided during the morning hours. The weight-lifting deck is near that spot, and as we worked we endured snide remarks from inmates whose sole aim in life was devoted to muscle.

The project at first appeared to be impossible as we hauled out one mammoth bag of weeds after another pulled from the first third of the elongated flower patch. But as we continued to pull out weeds with dirty hands, something magical began to happen. The harder we worked, the longer we worked, the more this garden project transformed our way of thinking. A feeling of calm descended over us as we toiled in the dirt. Perennial flowers began to reward our efforts with startling colors. Foot by square foot, we changed that little piece of the world into something truly beautiful. We replanted several of the flowers and cut back others. We turned the ground over, watered and fertilized the plants. We removed dozens of bags of weeds.

The two weeks turned into two months. When I paused in my weeding, I noticed for the first time that the insults had stopped. Instead, people were complimenting our work. I was not noticing the loudspeakers, nor was I aware of being in prison when gardening. I realized that I had incorporated gardening into my meditation practice. I was breathing in the scent of flowers and dirt and warm air. I was breathing out stress. I was feeling relaxed, and I could see that Shawn was feeling the same way.

Before long, paid workers began appearing asking to get involved. At first I felt territorial. Then I realized that this was another lesson the garden was freely offering. I became more aware of the negative power of attachments, grasping, and ego. I felt a deep sense of gratitude.

With each weed extracted from the ground, another flower was liberated, and slowly, so too were we.

POSTSCRIPTS

THE PRISONERS profiled felt proud to have their stories told and asked specifically to have their real names used, though the publisher insisted on changing them. Here is a follow-up on what happened to some of them.

BEN (in "Banana")
Ben was released in 2006 and returned to his home in the mid-West. He is trying to establish a home in the Southwest with relatives and he hopes to start a ranch.

BRAD (in "Soup")
Brad stayed in contact for a short time after release, but disappeared soon after moving to a large town in Washington.

BULLDOG
Bulldog sent cards for a few years after his release letting me know that he was happy to be home in Louisiana. The only complaint he had was about the heat. Bulldog told me he looks forward to Christmas each year.

CASEY (in "A Little Closer to Home")
Casey will be released from prison early in 2008. He has a solid release plan and will be living on the northern coast of Washington.

DERRICK
Derrick keeps coming back to prison or jail often. He is suffering deeply. It may take a few more years before Derrick realizes that there is another way to live his life.

HAROLD (in "Eyeball")
Harold remains in prison without chance of an early release.

MUNNY
Munny was released from INS in 1999. He lived with his mother in Portland, Oregon, for a few years. Munny received his GED and worked as the manager of a small store.

NORMAN (in "Entering the Way")
Norman was released from prison in 1998. He was immediately successful working with software companies. He has practiced with several Buddhist groups in the Seattle area.

ROBERT (in "Anger")
Robert is living in Seattle, Washington. He has struggled since his release in 2006 with all that is required by the State of those getting out on an early release. Even with a full-time job, he has barely enough money to eat after paying parole fees. Yet he is determined to make it at any cost.

RON (in "Essential Oil")
Ron was released from prison around 2001. He started a family, found a stable job at a warehouse, and was able to establish contact with his son.

SHAWN
Shawn was released in April 2007. He is actively involved in the Buddhist community in Spokane, Washington and is trying to help develop the Way-Home Project. Because of the trauma he endured in prison, health officials provided social services, including housing and other essentials. Shawn is constantly trying to make this world a better place, and has not forgotten the prison Sangha.

THAO (in "Reluctant Zen Master")
Thao had a difficult time upon release. He eventually resolved his immigration issues and enrolled in school. He often visited the Vietnamese temple in Seattle where he settled. Thao now has a family and is doing well.

UNNAMED INMATE (in "Metta")
The raging man who helped introduce me to Metta returned to prison often. Each time he appeared more aged and in greater suffering. He died in 2004 of a drug overdose.

THE WAY-HOME PROJECT

To avoid duplicating efforts, the Way-Home Project stopped assisting prisoners when the Paramita House was formed. In early 2007, the Paramita House closed, mostly due to the high volume of demand on its services and very limited resources. The Airway Heights Sangha is trying to revive the Way-Home Project to help their Sangha members with the transition from prison to society. We hope to establish a model that others can duplicate.

AUTHOR'S NOTE

THE PUBLISHER'S legal counsel felt that there could be liability if real names were used in the stories of inmates; accordingly all names of prisoners have been changed, to protect everyone. I was terribly disappointed about having to do this—the people about whom I write had, after all, enthusiastically granted permission to use their real names. News of the name changes brought to mind a well-known saying, "Shit happens." Though true enough, it's a saying I always thought to be crude and a kind of cop-out. I prefer to say, "It rains." Sometimes rain can be beneficial, and sometimes not. I wanted to use real names as a tribute to all those who laughed, cried, succeeded, failed, and learned with me throughout this experience. But in the end, it is more important to have these stories told than to have it my way.

APPENDIXES

I. THE FOUR NOBLE TRUTHS

THE TEACHINGS OF THE BUDDHA are simple and accessible to anyone. The Buddha recognized that human beings were ill with suffering and, like a physician, he diagnosed the illness, found out what caused it, determined how to cure it, and prescribed the treatment to make the patient well again.

If a person has a sore throat, a doctor may diagnose the illness as strep. The cause is an infection from streptococcus bacteria; the cure to take penicillin; the treatment three pills a day for ten days. The Buddha called the diagnosis, cause, cure, and treatment of human illness the Four Noble Truths. They are Noble because they come from deep wisdom and are deserving of respect. As in other teachings of the Buddha, the wording of the Four Noble Truths varies in different schools of Buddhism. The central idea, however, remains the same.

There are literally thousands of books written on Buddhism. These books may not be available to you, or you may have unlimited access to hundreds of books. In a way, it doesn't matter. If you understand the Four Noble Truths, you have the basics. Similarly, if you were told that it was raining outside, but you couldn't see or hear the rain, then you would not know if what you were told was the truth. If you went outside and got rained on, you would have the full realization that it was raining and would know for yourself the truth of the statement. The only way to know the truth of Buddhism is to experience it for yourself.

THE FIRST NOBLE TRUTH: SUFFERING

All beings suffer—this is the illness of living beings. If you are having a great day, knowing that it cannot last forever is suffering. Being in the midst of unpleasantness is suffering. Craving is suffering. Being away from what you like is suffering. Not getting what you want is suffering. Problems and disappointments are suffering. Ceaseless unfulfilled desires are suffering. And most of all, the impermanence of birth, old age, illness, and death are suffering. We suffer in life from the moment we are born. When we are sick, we are miserable. When old, we have aches and pains and our abilities fade. We fear death and feel sorrow when someone we love dies. The Buddha did not deny that there is happiness in life, but he pointed out that it does not last forever.

We all share the experience of suffering. To fully understand this is the first step toward freedom from suffering. Until the *illness* is diagnosed, the cure cannot be found.

THE SECOND NOBLE TRUTH: THE CAUSE OF SUFFERING

The Buddha said that the illness of living beings is suffering. He then went on to say that the cause of suffering is our selfish ego-based desires. Lustful cravings and passion, the desire for sensual experiences, wanting things to be the way *we* want them to be, all cause immense suffering. When things do not go our way, we lash out in anger and inflict pain on others. People are ignorant of the law of cause and effect and are greedy for the wrong kind of pleasures. They act in ways that are harmful to their bodies and peace of mind, and they cannot be satisfied or enjoy life. This is the *cause* of the illness of suffering.

THE THIRD NOBLE TRUTH: THE CESSATION OF SUFFERING

By cutting off greed, anger, and ignorance, we can end suffering. This means being willing to change our views and live in a more natural, moral, and peaceful way. It is akin to ending a dysfunctional relationship. Not until after the break do we realize how detrimental it had been all along. Buddhists call the state in which all suffering is ended true bliss, peace, joy. Everyone can attain this goal in this life with the help of the Buddha's teachings. This is the *cure* for the illness of suffering caused by craving.

THE FOURTH NOBLE TRUTH: THE EIGHTFOLD PATH FROM SUFFERING

The way out of suffering is called the Noble Eightfold Path. This is a path which helps us alter our delusive ideas and correct our world view. It is the *treatment* which implements the cure for the disease of suffering caused by selfish cravings.

THE NOBLE EIGHTFOLD PATH

The Buddhist symbol for the Noble Eightfold Path is a wheel with eight spokes, called the Wheel of Dharma. The Dharma means the teachings of the Buddha. The eight spokes represent the eight aspects of the Noble Eightfold Path. In the same way that every spoke is needed for the wheel to turn smoothly, we need to follow each step of the path.

Each of these steps is preceded by the word "right." This is because the Buddha recognized two kinds of intention, thought, and action. *Wrong action* is governed by desire, ill will, and harmfulness. It inevitably leads to pain and suffering for oneself and others. *Right action* is beneficial and altruistic, and leads to the growth of wisdom and compassion.

The Eightfold Path is divided into three sections: wisdom (the first two steps), morality (the third, fourth, and fifth steps), and concentration (the last three steps).

(1) Right Views—This means understanding the illusory nature of the ego-I. When we let go of our self-centered viewpoint, we see the world in an altogether different way, with enlightened understanding, wisdom, and compassion.

(2) Right Thought—Our thoughts affect our speech and actions. Even thinking about kindness and compassion has a powerful effect upon ourselves and upon others. The thought, which brings forth the aspiration and intention to change ourselves, is the first step to practicing Buddhism.

(3) Right Speech—Our speech reflects our thoughts. If we speak in a way that creates harmony, we help others and promote peace. Being mindful about our words keeps us from creating discord.

(4) Right Action—Our conduct and behavior should be in accord with our speech, thoughts, and views. Compassionate, selfless, skillful, ethical action alleviates suffering and helps others.

(5) Right Livelihood—This means engaging in an occupation that does not cause harm to others.

(6) Right Effort—We should put forth effort to practice the Dharma and to live in a caring, wise manner.

(7) Right Mindfulness (Awareness)—This means being aware of our thoughts, words, and deeds and being attentive in our life and in our interactions with others

(8) Right Concentration—This means meditation, focus, awareness. All aspects of the Eightfold Path spring from Right Concentration.

II. MEDITATION

MEDITATING IN PRISON is challenging. Slamming gates, loudspeakers throughout the day, piercing screams, random violence, cellmates, and inquisitive guards are not conducive to finding a time and place for silent introspection. Although it might seem that only accomplished meditators could overcome these obstacles, the fact is that thousands of people have learned how to meditate in prisons throughout the world.

In fact, it is precisely because of the difficulties and challenges that Buddhist practice and incarceration are an ideal combination. Everyday distractions and temptations are fewer in prison. There is an abundance of time available to practice. The stress and pressure of prison can act as teachings and an impetus for profound change, as well. But make no mistake, Buddhism requires diligent practice. People who achieve lofty aims in life do not attain them by sitting in front of a television set or playing card games all day. Likewise, people who wish to transform their lives need to make a dedicated effort to do so.

We are conditioned in this society to expect an instant fix while not bothering to contemplate that our flaws and manner of thinking took all our lives to develop and will take years of practice to change. When inmates attend Buddhist practice for the first time they are alarmed at having to be quiet without being able to pinball from one activity to another. But those who return over and over again are eventually transformed. They find what others say they want most of all: peace of mind and happiness.

This process can be long and arduous, but at the same time it is truly rewarding. You cannot become a great basketball player by lying in bed thinking about it. You have to go out on the court and practice basketball. If you want to develop muscles, you need to pump iron. To calm the mind, reduce your anger, increase your concentration, become aware, and learn to be happy, you must devote effort to the practice of meditation. Remember, though, meditation is not a competitive sport. It is better not to push for a specific result. Just sit and breathe. That is the first step.

There is no one ideal technique or a single method of meditation practice. Each of us approaches meditation from a different point of view. Put a red rose on a table and each person will see something different. For one person, the rose may represent a garden he worked in. For another it may conjure up memories of his mother. For another person a rose may be an irritating plant with thorns. We all bring a different perspective to every situation, and no one way is best for everyone. However, there are a few suggestions to facilitate the process of learning to meditate.

Many of these methods have been used for thousands of years, and are tried and true. Try one of the ancient meditation practices that have been handed down by enlightened masters before attempting to create your own. Nonetheless, if you have found something that works to calm your mind and help you relax, then by all means go for it. It is a good idea after trying meditation on your own for a while to seek out a teacher or at a minimum read the meditation manuals available to prisoners upon request. Help is always available. Don't be afraid to ask for it—it's a real shortcut!

GETTING STARTED

Do what you can to create an environment most conducive to relaxation. Find a time of day when there is the least distraction—very early in the morning and late at night are good times. Try to practice at the same time each day, twice if possible. There is no set amount of time for meditation, but most people find it easiest to start with ten to fifteen minutes and work up from there. Generally speaking it is advisable not to sit for more than thirty to forty minutes at a time without moving.

Pick a place that has no draft and is not too cold or hot—though in truth, it's possible to do meditation anywhere. Wear loose-fitting clothes. If you do not have a meditation cushion and meditation mat, fold a blanket into a padded mat. Sit on it, buttocks slightly elevated from the floor with legs crossed in a comfortable position, perhaps with one leg in front of or over the other leg. Make sure you have padding for your ankles and try to have your knees on the floor. You can also try a kneeling posture by straddling a cushion, pillow, or blanket. If you have back or knee problems or if you are unable to sit on the floor in this way, try sitting in a chair. Sit toward the front edge of the seat with your back away from the backrest. If no chair is available, sit on the edge of your bed or bunk. Remember, you get no points for looking cool or for pain endurance—don't twist yourself up into a pretzel for no reason!

The important thing is to get comfortable with your back straight without forcing the posture. The correct posture will come naturally with practice. Your shoulders should be even and not slouched forward. Relax your mouth, but keep it closed. Your head should be erect: your nose in line with your navel, your ears in line with your shoulders.

Keep your eyes slightly closed, looking down at a 45-degree angle. Try to avoid closing your eyes entirely or staring straight ahead. Although some people meditate with their eyes closed, it is not ideal because you can easily fall asleep. The mind also tends to wander more readily when the eyes are closed. Keeping the eyes slightly open helps to bring your meditation into your daily life.

Try to make your place of meditation as welcoming as possible. For example, you might like to place a picture of the Buddha, Jesus, or a favorite deity in front of you for inspiration or arrange photos of nature, a flower or fruit or something else, or nothing, if you prefer. Experiment so that you find a way to be comfortable and not easily distracted. If you can do all this and put a slight smile on your face, you are in one of the most ideal positions for meditation.

Once you find the posture you like most, then it is time to try one of the more effective means used to calm the mind, quiet the incessant mental chatter we all experience, and learn to relax and meditate. There are countless effective methods, and you may come up with something other than the suggestions in this book that work for you. Look for a way to calm your mind so that meditation is possible. Remember that the first stage of meditation is quiet stillness, free of activity. Advanced meditation is quietness in the *midst* of activity—but this can take years of practice to achieve.

When you have finished meditating, before you get up and move, bring your awareness back to your breath. Now bow to your altar, image, or wall, or bow simply to stretch your back. Get a feel of your body to make sure your legs have not fallen asleep while you were sitting. Get up slowly, mindfully, and observe how peaceful you feel. By taking this mental holiday you have made it possible for your mind to deal with your surroundings in a more serene, effective manner.

Try not to think too much about what you should be feeling or experiencing. Try not to let your mind play with thoughts. Don't worry about what you will be doing after you have finished practicing. The future gets here so soon that you don't have time to think about it anyway. Just relax and experiment with one of these methods.

METHODS OF MEDITATION

COUNTING THE BREATH

When you first begin meditation you will probably experience many thoughts and feelings rising to your consciousness. Counting the breath introduces you to the practice of meditation and helps you establish a rhythm. This ancient method is by far the most straightforward, practical, and effective means to calm and focus the mind. It is commonly given as the initial practice to beginners in many schools of meditation, but it is also used by advanced practitioners.

With hands palm down on the knees or placed in your lap palms up, left hand on top of the right, with the tips of your thumbs lightly touching, breathe in deeply, and as you exhale count *one*. Try not to think of anything. Instead, focus on that single breath. As you continue focusing on the breath, extend the count to the absolute end of the breath: *o-o-o-o-n-n-n-n-e-e-e-e*. Inhale, and as you exhale count *two*, again, extending the mental count throughout the entire length of the breath. Continue like this until you get to ten, then go back to one again. If along the way your mind begins to act like a monkey swinging from branch to branch, stop, smile at the monkey mind, and begin again with *one*. Breathe in, breathe out, *o-o-o-o-n-n-n-n-e-e-e-e*. Breathe in, breathe out, *tw-o-o-o-o-o-o*. And continue on.

Most people have trouble getting past three at first. Try it. It is not a contest! Do not be hard on yourself. Just keep trying. That is why they call it practice. Eventually you will get to four or five before a distracting thought arises. Then you will get to eight or even nine without thinking of anything and then your mind will congratulate you for getting that far or you will begin thinking about your pet or something will pop up and that is when you stop, smile, and begin again. Keep trying this. Like anything else you will get better at it with practice.

As you become more experienced, your awareness will become more subtle. You will be less bound by expectations and will be more mindful. In time, you will be able to let go of the false identity of "I" and your mind will open to the universe in all its possibilities. Until such time, sit quietly, patiently, attentively. When thoughts arise do not struggle with them, just gently set them aside. Breathe in air, breathe out calm, and don't forget to smile at the wonder of it all. The rest will come when you least expect it.

COMPRESSED PRACTICE

A common remark made by beginners is the difficulty of sitting quietly for an extended period of time. Sitting down for twenty to forty minutes with the mind swirling and joints aching can be discouraging for anyone, all the more so if you don't have the advice and support of a teacher. One solution is to learn how to sit in smaller bites. It's a kind of "compressed practice."

Try sitting for five minutes. Breathe in, focusing on the air coming into your nostrils. Breathe out all the air you can and count that as one. Keep that up to the count of ten then get up and mindfully stretch. Stand still for a moment and sit again for another session of five minutes. If thoughts arise during your breath counts, do not get frustrated. It is only the old monkey mind trying to interfere. Do this compressed practice over and over again for as long as you like for up to half an hour. Try this consistently and you will find that you are able to sit for longer periods and with less strain.

MINDFULNESS

Mindfulness lets us see the world as it is rather than as we wish it to be. It is not necessary to sit on a cushion in front of an altar to practice mindfulness. Anyone can do it anytime, anywhere. Being mindful requires us to pay attention to what we say, think, and do. The more we go through that process, the more we become aware of past actions that were harmful or at the very least selfish. Mindfulness places our deeds under a microscope for scrutinizing without the distortion of illusion. It dissolves our idealized view of ourselves and completely exposes us.

It is mindfulness that makes it possible to free ourselves from having a shameful past by enabling us to live in the present moment. When we do that, we are more aware of our actions. We pay close attention to what we do, say, and even think, and because of this we are improving what will happen to us in the future.

How do we practice mindfulness? Mindfully going to shave, I breathe in, I breathe out. Mindfully lathering my face, I breathe in, I breathe out. Mindfully I begin to shave. I breathe in, I breathe out. I nick myself, a dot of blood appears. How easily I forget to be mindful. Mindfully I wipe the blood from my cheek. I breathe in, I breathe out.

WATER-DIRT MEDITATION

This method is particularly effective for those who need a visual tool to help in the meditation process. Don't try it, though, if it means being sent to segregation or getting an infraction!

Take a small, empty, clear plastic jar and put three or four heaping spoons of dirt in it. Fill the rest of the jar with water. When you are ready to meditate, vigorously shake the jar and set it slightly in front of you. Rest your eyes on the jar and imagine that your mind is like the contents of the jar: a mass of swirling thoughts and concepts and chatter. Remember to breathe deeply, but naturally. Keep your eyes on the jar and observe as the dirt settles. As the water becomes clearer, so will your mind. When you become angry, it is like shaking up that jar of dirt and water. Your mind becomes cloudy and confused. If you sit calmly and breathe deeply, your anger will settle calmly like dirt in water. Try this at least twice if possible. Keep in mind that if the dirt is fine it may take a while to settle. That's okay. After all, the one thing prisoners have in abundance is time.

SOUND MEDITATION

Get comfortable and sit in your preferred posture. If you have a clock, focus on the ticking of the clock. Four or five ticks for the in-breath, three or four ticks for the out-breath. Each time thoughts invade your mind, stop, smile at the thought, then start again. You get no medals, no one will criticize you, there are no judges. Just you and the clock. Other sounds can be utilized as well. When a gate slams loudly, stop whatever you are doing and use what could be an irritating noise as a reminder to practice a mindfulness exercise by breathing in and smiling. Thank the sound for slowing you down and allowing you to be present and attentive. Then, for a few seconds, breathe in deeply and breathe out. Try not to think about the task or activity you were just involved in. Allow yourself to be present. By doing this type of exercise with sounds, you transform your thinking and attitude about things you consider to be negative. Loud noises are part of prison life. If you can make them work for you, then you are well on the way to developing a strong meditation practice.

PEBBLE MEDITATION

Often people come to prison with depression, hyperactivity, or attention deficit disorder. It is so difficult for them to calm their mind that they give up trying or never start. For such people, sitting still can pose as great a challenge as dealing with the problems that meditation helps solve. If you feel that this describes you, this simple tool to calm the mind might be helpful.

Collect ten pebbles or ten other small objects. Find a comfortable place to sit. Perhaps you can use the cell when everyone is elsewhere or asleep. Place the pebbles at arm's length in front of you. Sit up, inhale and exhale three times deeply. Then slowly, mindfully, lean forward, breathe in, and pick up a pebble. Now sit upright while exhaling and place the pebble beside you. Repeat this process until all the pebbles are gathered together near you. Then pick up one of the pebbles, inhale, lean forward and place it in front of you at arms' length. Repeat this until all of the pebbles are back where they started. Sit upright. Breathe deeply three times and smile at your practice. Observe how you feel. Do this every day at more or less the same time for two to three weeks. When you think you are ready, try one of the other exercises mentioned here or any meditation method you know. You will find that your body and mind respond well to being more relaxed and calm.

WALKING MEDITATION

Most prisoners walk every day. Whether it is walking to the chow hall, going to the medical clinic, the library, getting to work, or walking the exercise yard, the opportunity to practice is there.

You cannot walk normally and match your breath with each step. That would be too slow for prison officials. Instead, try breathing in while taking three steps and breathing out while taking three steps. Or just bring your awareness to your feet and to the process of walking. Pay attention as you move your legs with each step. If you know a chant or have a favorite mantra you might use that while walking in the yard. With practice you will discover how many steps are necessary to finish a particular chant. If you do this every day, you will learn that there are a certain number of chants you can do in one circumambulation of the yard. You can do the same thing in your cell. Or you can circle your cell slowly, matching your step to each breath.

You have to breathe to stay alive, and most people have to walk to get from place to place. You might as well use these necessities to deepen your practice. Be creative. Find ways to include sound, lights, or even your cell space in your practice. Officers have to count prisoners at least three times a day in most prisons. This is usually done at the same time every day. Fifteen to thirty minutes before each time the officers call for count, begin your practice. When count is called use that as your gong to end the practice. See what works for you.

TEA MEDITATION

The simple act of making tea can be a profound meditation practice. All day long we decide to do one task or another without giving much thought to what we are doing. If you do something, do it wholeheartedly. If you wish to make tea, try mindful tea making. Take a cloth or paper towel and place it on the table or floor. On that, put all your tea ingredients. Make the hot water being mindful of where the water came from and the miracle of water. Sit down with the hot water and tea ingredients and steep your tea attentively. Think of the tea growing in the sun and the minerals that help make tea. Think about the people who harvest the tea leaves and how it got to you. Smile at the rain that kept the ground moist and the vendors who sold you the tea. If you were able to think of everything connected with your tea it would take forever, because the tea contains everything in the universe. After a reasonable amount of time dedicated to mindful tea making, begin mindful tea drinking. Sip your tea slowly, and taste the universe.

SMILING PRACTICE

Smiling is an easy exercise and normally comes naturally to people. In prison, though, smiles are rare, which is why smiling in prison is a practice that requires some work. It is far easier to get and give frowns and dour looks than to smile. The surest way to reverse frowning trends is to mindfully smile at the frozen people who rarely if ever smile. From there, smile at the morning, at the food, at the people near you, and at every situation possible. Do this for a day and two things will happen: your face will ache from the continued effort and you will sleep peacefully.

If you don't already smile most of the time, or if you have to think about smiling before you do it, then smiling practice is a great way to begin meditation. Since there are more muscles involved in maintaining a frown than a smile, it makes sense to smile. Smiling practice is a delightful way to set the tone for the entire day and it also helps dissolve barriers and remove obstacles.

When you wake up, don't do anything until you smile. When you go to the bathroom, smile while urinating. Smile at your reflection in the mirror and smile while combing your hair and washing your face—not a big cheesy grin, but a gentle smile that adds light to your eyes. Smile at every "first" in your day. When you first walk out the door, when you first see a meal, when you first see your boss and co-workers. Smile at the razor wire, smile at the concrete. Within the radiance of your true smile everything will be embraced. Give your friend a warm smile, he or she needs it. Give the person you dislike a warm smile, he or she needs it as well. At the end of your day as you lie down in your bed, smile at your dreams and you will know that your smiling day was, beyond a doubt, delightful.

LOVING-KINDNESS MEDITATION

In prison, there are a lot of raw emotions running around, both internally and externally. When you become more mindful, you will be aware of these emotions, begin to understand where they come from, and recognize which are helpful and which are not. In so doing, you will be more in control and will not be at the mercy of your feelings. One way to achieve this awareness is the practice of loving-kindness meditation.

Sit comfortably in a quiet spot. If you have one, place a mirror in front of you so that you can see your face. Breathe in and out deeply three times. Think of the person in the mirror who once was a baby. Extend loving thoughts out to that baby saying: "May you be happy. May you be well. May you be free from distress. May you find peace." Think of the face in the mirror as a child learning to ride a bike.

Extend loving-kindness to that child. See the face in the mirror as an adolescent showing signs of independence. Extend loving-kindness to that child. Think of the face in the mirror as a young teenager going into high school. Extend to him loving-kindness. Look at the face in the mirror and see the person reflected there as a young adult. Extend to him loving-kindness. Continue to do this until you reach your current age. Say to yourself, "May I be happy. May I be well. May I be free from distress. May I be filled with peace and love."

Look at your present face and forgive yourself for all your past transgressions. Extend to yourself loving-kindness. Breathe in and out deeply. Smile. Then think of those you love most. Extend to them your caring and offer them loving-kindness. Think of the friends you have and do the same for them. Breathe in, breathe out deeply as you do this. Think of people you do not know well. Offer them kind thoughts. Think of all those you do not like. Forgive them for their actions and offer them thoughts of loving-kindness. Finally, think of your greatest enemies or those who did you great harm. Breathe deeply, smile, and offer them the same loving-kindness you offered to those you love most. Smile into the mirror, and say, "May all beings be happy. May all beings be well. May all being be free from distress. May all beings find peace."

FINAL THOUGHTS ON MEDITATION

Our minds are busy from the time we wake up in the morning until we fall asleep at night. We spend the entire day chasing thoughts. In meditation, we learn to pay attention to what is in our minds. Eventually, we notice that thoughts do not flow from one to the other like river water. A thought ends and another begins and in between is a split second of quiet. Meditation can increase the duration of these moments and allow our mind to rest. There will be occasions when you have thoughts and mental formations that are distracting. Try to recognize them for what they are and gently ignore them without playing with that particular thought. Bring your attention back to the stillness of your calm mind and continue with your practice.

It takes calmness, patience, and a certain degree of faith to practice every day. The changes we may be seeking are so subtle and gradual that progress can be imperceptible. Do not berate yourself for failing to immediately see the changes taking place within. Know that your practice is testimony to the fact that you have the courage to embark upon the most demanding endeavor of your life as well as the most reward-ing. Be heartened by the fact that you are willing to examine core beliefs and endure what may be painful insights in order to experience the inner transformation necessary to out-wardly change our behaviors.

Practice has its own dynamics and rhythms—no two peri-ods of meditation are identical. Calmly persevere by gently working through all that practice offers. In time, you will find that engaging in practice is the most comfortable, fasci-nating, natural thing to do.

Nothing could be more worthwhile than taking time out of each day to get away from the card games, the television, the war stories, and the negativity and just be with yourself, cultivating your mind, calming your mind, and learning to be happy.

III. RECOMMENDED READING

THERE ARE SO MANY wonderful Buddhist books available today that it is impossible to name the ideal book for the beginner. If you are new to Buddhism these books are a great way to start and are excellent to read over and over again.

Being Peace, by Thich Nhat Hanh, Parallax Press

Three Pillars of Zen: Teaching, Practice, Enlightenment, by Philip Kapleau, Knopf Publishing

Mindfulness in Plain English, by Bhante Henepola Gunaratana, Wisdom Publications

Zen Meditation in Plain English, by John Daishin Buksbazen, Wisdom Publications

How to Practice: The Way to a Meaningful Life, by H. H. The Dalai Lama, Simon & Schuster

Sitting Inside, Buddhist Practice in America's Prisons, by Kobai Scott Whitney, Prison Dharma Network

Buddhism for Beginners, by Thubten Chodron, Snow Lion Publications

The Tibetan Book of Living and Dying: The Spiritual Classic & International Bestseller, by Sogyal Rinpoche, HarperCollins Publishers

Lord of the Dance: Autobiography of a Tibetan Lama, by H. E. Chagdud Tulku Rinpoche, Padma Publishing

How to Meditate: A Practical Guide, by Kathleen McDonald, Wisdom Publications

Milking the Painted Cow: The Creative Power of Mind and the Shape of Reality in Light of the Buddhist Tradition, by Tarthang Tulku, Dharma Publishing

Transforming Adversity into Joy and Courage: An Explanation of the Thirty-Seven Practices of Bodhisattvas, by Geshe Jampa Tegchok, Snow Lion Publications

Finding the Still Point: A Beginner's Guide to Meditation, by John Daido Loori, Shambhala Publications

Don't-Know Mind: The Spirit of Korean Zen, by Richard Shrobe, Shambhala Publications

Mindfulness Yoga: The Awakened Union of Body, Breath, and Mind, by Frank Jude Boccio, Wisdom Publications

Hardcore Zen: Punk Rock, Monster Movies, and the Truth About Reality, by Brad Warner, Wisdom Publications

Many books are available at little or no cost to prisoners. Please refer to the *Resource Guide* for more information.

IV. RESOURCE GUIDE

LITERATURE

Amitabha Buddhist Society of U.S.A.
650 South Bernardo Ave.
Sunnyvale, CA 94087
Tel: (408) 736–3386
E-mail: info@amtb-usa.org
Web: www.amtb-usa.org
Pure Land Buddhism (Mahayana).
Audio, video tapes, books, and pictures of
the Buddha.
Write for a catalog. Provide specific prison
guidelines for receiving items.

BUDDHIST ASSOCIATION OF THE
UNITED STATES
    2020 Route 301
    Carmel, NY 10512
    Tel: (845) 228–4287
    E-mail: Bausbook@aol.com
    Web: www.baus.org
    Mahayana and Theravada, no Tibetan books.

BUDDHIST BOOKSTORE
    1710 Octavia St.
    San Francisco, CA 94109
    E-mail: bcahq@pacbell.net

BUDDHIST PEACE FELLOWSHIP
    P.O. Box 4650
    Berkeley, CA 94704–0650
    E-mail: prisons@bpf.org
    Web: www.bpf.org
    Publishes *Turning Wheel Journal.*
    Reduced rate for prisoners ($10).

DHARMA PUBLISHING
    2910 San Pablo Ave.
    Berkeley, CA 94702
    Tel: (510) 548–5407
    E-mail: info@dharmapublishing.com
    Web: www.dharmapublishing.com
    Prefer sending books to prison libraries.
    Will send books to individuals.

GASSHO NEWSLETTER
Atlanta Soto Zen Center
Attn: Gassho
1167-C Zonolite Place
Atlanta, GA 30306
Web: www.aszc.org
Newsletter is created by and written for incarcerated
Buddhists.
Write to be placed on mailing list. They welcome
articles, artwork, etc., for publication.

THE HEART MOUNTAIN PROJECT
1223 South St., Francis Drive, Suite C
Santa Fe, NM 87505
17-page meditation manual free of charge to
prisoners.
Spanish translation is available.

LAMA YESHE WISDOM ARCHIVE
P.O. Box 356
Weston, MA 02493
Web: www.lamayeshe.com
Extensive collection of Tibetan Buddhist books free
to prisoners.

LIBERATION PRISON PROJECT
P.O. Box 31527
San Francisco, CA 94131
Tel: (415) 701–8500
E-mail: info@liberationprisonproject.org
Web: www.liberationprisonproject.org
Tibetan Buddhism. Free books and materials for prisoners.
Free subscription to *Liberation Magazine*.
Literature also available in Spanish, Vietnamese, and Chinese.

MINDFUL BUDDHA OUTREACH PROJECT
1753 Oxford Dr. #3
Cheyenne, WY 82001
E-mail: Mindfulbuddha@hotmail.com
Pen-pals, books, CDs, audio tapes on Buddhism and meditation.

NALJOR PRISON DHARMA SERVICE
P.O. Box 7417
Boulder, CO 80306–7417
E-mail: npds@naljor.us
Web: www.naljorprisondharmaservice.org
Offers the *Heart of Dharma Collection*.
Entire collection for a cost of eight first-class stamps.

NATIONAL BUDDHIST PRISON SANGHA
Zen Mountain Monastery
P.O. Box 197, South Plank Rd.
Mt. Tremper, NY 12457
Books, audio tapes, and personal guidance in Zen Buddhism.

PARALLAX PRESS
P.O. Box 7355
Berkeley, CA 94707
Teaching by Thich Nhat Hanh.
Books available free of charge to prisoners.
Write for catalog.

PRISON DHARMA NETWORK
P.O. Box 4623
Boulder, CO 80306
Tel: (650) 952–9513
E-mail: pdn@indra.com
Web: www.prisonDharmaNetwork.org

SUPPORT NETWORK FOR PRISONERS
Prison Library Project
915 West Foothill Blvd., Suite C128
Claremont, CA 91711
Publishes *Sitting Inside: Buddhist Practice in
America's Prisons.*
Specify what types of books you would like. Free
resource guide upon request.

SHAMBHALA PUBLICATIONS
Horticultural Hall
300 Massachusetts Ave.
Boston, MA 02115–4544
Tel: 1–888–424–2329
Web: www.Shambhala.com

SNOW LION PUBLICATIONS
P.O. Box 6483
Ithaca, NY 14851–6483
E-mail: info@snowlionpub.com
Web: www.snowlionpub.com
Free newsletter and catalog upon request.

TREASURE VALLEY DHARMA FRIENDS
Ven. Thubten Chodron
P.O. Box 9126
Boise, ID 83703–9126
Tibetan Tradition. Happy to send tapes of guided
meditation and books.

VERMONT ZEN CENTER
P.O. Box 880
Shelburne, VT 05482
E-mail: vzcinfo@att.net
Web: www.vermontzen.org
Free newsletter upon request.

WISDOM PUBLICATIONS
199 Elm St.
Somerville, MA.02144
E-mail: info@wisdompubs.org
Web: www.wisdompubs.org
Publishes large selection of Buddhist books.

BUDDHIST SUPPLIES

DHARMA CRAFTS
405 Waltham St.
Suite 234
Lexington, MA 02421
Order Toll Free: 1–800–794–9862
Web: www.dharmacrafts.com

DHARMA WARE
54 E. Tinker St.
Woodstock, NY 12498
Mail order: 1–888–679–4900

TIBETAN TREASURES
Chagdud Gonpa Foundation
P.O. Box 279
Junction City, CA 96048–0279
Tel: (877) 479–6129
Web: www.tibetantreasures.com

TENZING MOMO INC.
Eric Pollard
93 Pike St.
Seattle, WA 98101

TIBETAN SPIRIT
P.O. Box 57
Boonsboro, MD 21713
Toll free: 1–888–327–2890
E-mail: shop@tibetanspirit.com
Web: www.tibetanspirit.com

SAMADHI CUSHIONS
Dept. SS
30 Church St.
Barnet, VT 05821
Tel: 1–800–331–7751

ZIJI
9148 Kerry Rd.
Boulder, CO 80303
Tel: 1–800–565–8470
E-mail: ziji@csd.net

NIPPON KODO CO.-LTD.
(Incense mostly)
Los Angeles office
2771 Plaza del Amo, Suite 806
Torrace, CA 90503
E-mail: nktoyo@nifty.com
Web: www.nipponkodo.com

THE MONASTERY STORE
Dharma Communications
P.O. Box 156
Mount Tremper, NY 12457
Tel: (845) 688–7993
Web: www.dharma.net
20% discount for prisoners.

ABOUT THE AUTHOR

CALVIN MALONE was born in Munich, Germany, in 1951 to a German mother and an American father. At the age of seven he and his family moved to Monterey, California, and Calvin entered the second grade, speaking only German. Within a year he was fluent in English.

Calvin attended Walla Walla Community College and studied European History. He also traveled extensively throughout Europe.

Calvin began practicing Buddhism soon after he entered prison and started writing about his prison experiences shortly thereafter. He has published numerous articles in Buddhist magazines and newsletters. He was instrumental in developing a post-prison transitional program and makes malas (prayer beads) for Buddhist prisoners around the country. Calvin is currently working on a Buddhist novel.

Calvin was incarcerated in 1992 with a 20-year sentence for aggravated assault. He is scheduled for early release from prison in October 2009.

About Wisdom Publications

WISDOM PUBLICATIONS, a nonprofit publisher, is dedicated to making available authentic works relating to Buddhism for the benefit of all. We publish books by ancient and modern masters in all traditions of Buddhism, translations of important texts, and original scholarship. Additionally, we offer books that explore East-West themes unfolding as traditional Buddhism encounters our modern culture in all its aspects. Our titles are published with the appreciation of Buddhism as a living philosophy, and with the special commitment to preserve and transmit important works from Buddhism's many traditions.

To learn more about Wisdom, or to browse books online, visit our website at www.wisdompubs.org.

You may request a copy of our catalog online or by writing to this address:

Wisdom Publications
199 Elm Street
Somerville, Massachusetts 02144 USA
Telephone: 617-776-7416
Fax: 617-776-7841
Email: info@wisdompubs.org
www.wisdompubs.org

THE WISDOM TRUST

As a nonprofit publisher, Wisdom is dedicated to the publication of Dharma books for the benefit of all sentient beings and dependent upon the kindness and generosity of sponsors in order to do so. If you would like to make a donation to Wisdom, you may do so through our website or our Somerville office. If you would like to help sponsor the publication of a book, please write or email us at the address above.

Thank you.

Wisdom is a nonprofit, charitable 501(c)(3) organization affiliated with the Foundation for the Preservation of the Mahayana Tradition (FPMT).